TAVUA

THE WHITE CANNIBAL

TAVUA

THE WHITE CANNIBAL

BY RICK WILLIAMSON

Verlag Angelika Hörnig

TAVUA
THE WHITE CANNIBAL

by Rick Williamson

Photos by Rick Williamson

Cover design by Brigitte Löcher and Rick Williamson

Realization and Layout by Brigitte Löcher

Lecturer: Mitch Cohen

Printed in Germany
by Laub GmbH & Co. KG

ISBN: 978-3-938921-05-0

Published by
Verlag Angelika Hörnig
Siebenpfeiffferstr. 18
D-67071 Ludwigshafen
Germany
www.bogenschiessen.de
www.archery.de

Dedication

To my parents, Derek and Doreen,
and all the selfless people I met during my travels.

The following events occurred over a ten-year period
that ended in September 2005.

Introduction

It wasn't until I was thirty-five and I became a photojournalist that I discovered members of my family were hardcore explorers. I was amazed when my father and my uncle told me they'd been part of historic expeditions in the Arctic and the Australian desert, but what really fascinated me was their humbleness and why they'd kept their unique experiences to themselves for so long. Many people would think that's an unnatural thing to do, but what is normal? Why do we act in certain ways, and what is it that makes us truly human?

One of the oldest questions man has asked is what happens when we die. I've always been fascinated by primitive cultures that believe in the supernatural and the way they seem to have an appreciation of the human consciousness that science still doesn't understand. I decided to try to find some of the answers to the difficult questions we have about ourselves, by stepping back through time and exploring the untainted minds of primitive people who still lived as our ancestors did thousands of years ago.

Nowadays, finding a primitive tribe that's never been documented before is a rarity. During my first expedition as a photojournalist I walked across Vanuatu's largest island, Espiritu Santo, and discovered a legendary tribe of cannibalistic pygmies living deep in the jungle in the rugged highlands. They were naturally violent, hated the white man, and killed any outsiders who foolishly entered their territory.
The name of their village, **Winea** means "**to eat man**," so it's hardly surprising that no one else had been able to record their complex culture. After I was initiated into a neighbouring clan that shares the same language and customs as Winea, while I studied these fascinating people I was completely at their mercy each time I immersed myself in their cruel and unsympathetic society.

Some of the mystical beliefs and bizarre rituals that I documented on Santo are so deeply rooted in the culture they have evolved from, and are so way beyond the boundaries of our thinking, most outsiders would find it impossible to accept they are a reality. After I crossed a massive cultural divide and gained total acceptance, I was given a unique insight into the highlander's remarkable culture and found the answers I was looking for.

This book isn't written by an expert, but it is written by someone who has witnessed what no other civilized man has seen or would ever want to see. It's a "warts and all" account of my personal journey and the startling new discoveries that I made. I faced life-threatening rituals and became a paramount chief and a cannibal so that I have the right to share secret customs with you. I've included events and rites that I didn't witness myself, to provide a clearer picture of what I did see and to give you a better understanding of how primitive peoples see themselves.

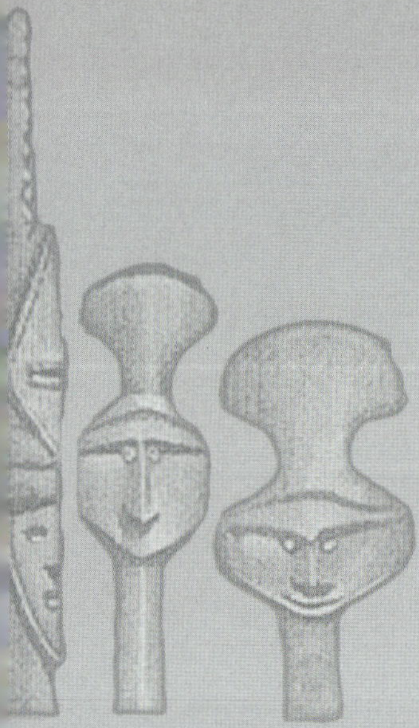

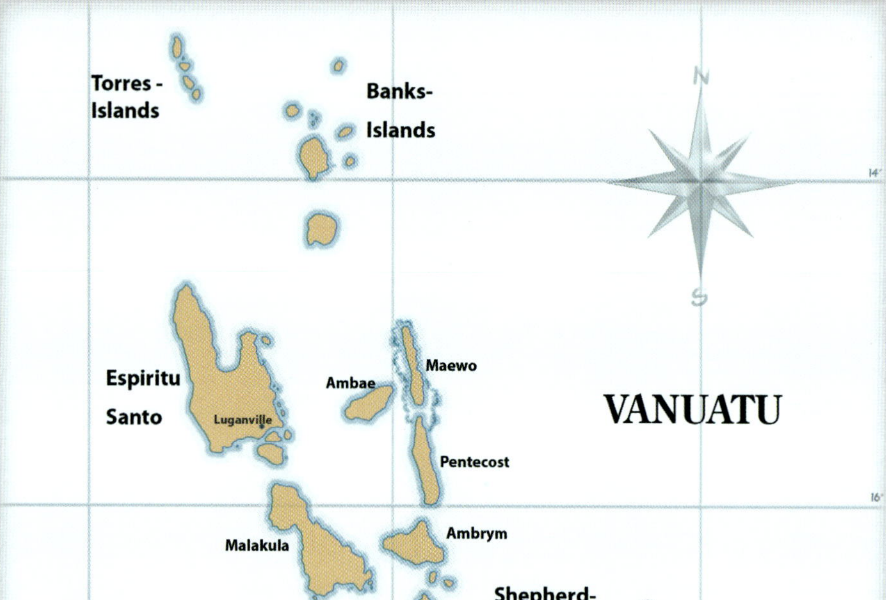
Torres -
Islands
Banks-
Islands
N
S
14°
Espiritu
Santo
Luganville
Ambae
Maewo
VANUATU
Pentecost
16°
Malakula
Ambrym
Shepherd-
Islands
CORAL SEA
SOUTH PACIFIC OCEAN
Efate
Port Vila
18°
Erromango
Tanna
Anatom
170°

PAPUA
NEW GUINEA
Vanuatu
AUSTRALIA
SYDNEY
NEW
ZEALAND

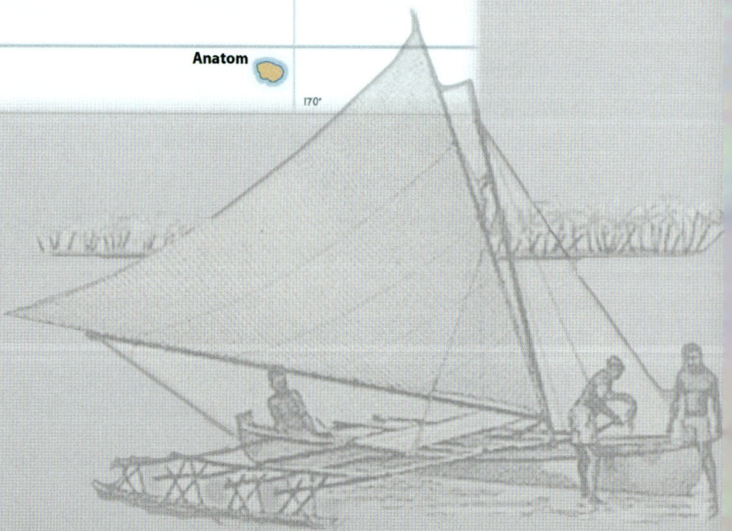

Beginner's Luck

Before I became a photojournalist, I travelled to some of the most captivating and inaccessible places on the planet. I explored remote jungles, lived with primitive tribes, and became an incurable nomad who wanted life to be a succession of exciting adventures. Sometimes it felt like I was being sucked towards my destiny. I constantly wanted to step off the tainted world civilization has created, so that I could experience the other timeless and mystical world of primitive man.

In the past I'd made brief stopovers in Vanuatu and vowed to visit its beautiful outer islands and primitive peoples. Once I started delving into the archipelago's remarkable history I quickly realised this was the perfect place to start my new career.
Vanuatu consists of a Y shaped chain of islands running in a north-south direction across the Pacific Ocean, 170 kilometres south of its nearest neighbour, the Solomon Islands.

Before Vanuatu gained independence in 1980, it was called the New Hebrides and was jointly governed as a British and French condominium. When the word Vanuatu is translated, depending on which indigenous language is being used, it means "our land" or "the country that stands up." Vanuatu also stands out due to its tremendous cultural and religious diversity. Around one hundred and fifteen different dialects are spoken, and each island has its own artistic styles and beliefs.

Vanuatu's geography is as diverse as its fascinating cultures. Some of the stunning scenery was created by violent geological upheavals, and in many respects its people are also a product of harsh disruptions. They haven't enjoyed a gentle transition from the past into the present. During the nineteenth century the Melanesians were invaded by the Church, blackbirders (slave traders), colonial settlers, and worst of all, introduced diseases. Depopulation occurred at an alarming rate.
In 1800 Vanuatu had an estimated one million inhabitants, but only one year later measles had eliminated a staggering one-third of the entire population.
By the turn of the twentieth century less than 100,000 people remained, and in 1935 only a dismal 45,000 natives were thought to have survived the devastating epidemics. After being physically decimated they faced another foreign scourge when a steady stream of evangelists started destroying their beliefs.

Nowadays, fish, beef, copra, and cocoa are the main exports, but Vanuatu's biggest asset is its hospitable people. Most of the population are Melanesians, and all indigenous inhabitants are called Ni-Vanuatu. Tourism remains the largest source of foreign income, but very few visitors travel to the remote outer islands.

There aren't many books that cover the archipelago's turbulent history. A few anthropologists and interested missionaries managed to document its fascinating past, when cannibalistic tribes practised human sacrifice, sorcery was rampant, and everyday life revolved around unusual rituals. The more I read, the more captivated I became. I purposely avoided islands that have been studied by anthropologists, and decided to walk across rugged Espiritu Santo (also known as Santo), to try to make contact with the country's most isolated and primitive inhabitants. That decision would change my life forever.

When I read that black magic was thought to be at the very core of Santo's traditional religions, it enhanced the island's mystique and appeal. This was the perfect destination for a fledgling photojournalist, where I'd explore the true Vanuatu and where maybe startling discoveries still lay hidden in the depths of the jungle or in its people's minds.

Tourism is vital to Vanuatu's growth. Travellers regularly visit cultures whose traditions kill or injure their own people in order to maintain social harmony, and to punish those who bring shame upon their beliefs. Although uninvited visitors to Santo's interior are greeted with an instinctive antagonism, the rest of Vanuatu is by far the safest country I've worked in.

This fascinating archipelago offers unique eco-tourism, and has friendly peoples with vibrant cultures. Don't let my unique experiences put you off going there. Without a doubt, working in Vanuatu has been one of the highlights of my life.

When I arrived at Vanuatu's capital, Port Vila, I met with Ralph Regenvanu, the director of the Cultural Centre and Museum. He gave me an official letter of introduction and said I could try to use one of his fieldworkers on Santo as a guide. I was extremely grateful, but realistically the letter had little value.

Santo is only 4,010 square kilometres in size, but because the highlanders have such a violent reputation, a field worker has never visited the villages in the rugged interior, and as a consequence, the Cultural Centre didn't have any archival material about the people's customs.

While I was buying my tickets to fly to Santo, the manager of the domestic airline, Van Air, said he'd heard rumours about a legendary pygmy tribe that lived deep in the jungle. If I could find a sacred conch shell nestled in a banyan tree and blew it a couple of times, the tiny cannibals would be drawn to the sound. I'd read that pygmies lived in the highlands about one hundred years ago, and had become extinct; but instead of completely ignoring some of the obviously exaggerated stories, I felt there might be an element of truth to them. It made me even more determined to explore the island.

Several days later I flew to Santo and landed just as dusk enveloped Luganville airport in darkness. While I was looking for a taxi and asking for directions I met John Noel. He offered to give me a ride, threw my well-travelled pack onto the back of his battered pickup, and as we rattled along the road into town, he said I could stay with his family.

John wore a huge halo of bushy hair, and had a slight middle-aged physique that seemed to contradict his reputation for being a tough politician and a hard-nosed chief. He was quick to mention everyone knew about his political status, even the reclusive villagers in the remote highlands. The police also knew him well. They'd imprisoned him several times for inciting politically motivated riots. He became a close, trustworthy friend, but was the sort of man I'd hate to have as an enemy.

When we arrived at his home, his wife and children treated me like one of the family. After I showed them photos I'd taken in the Solomons and Irian Jaya, John looked worried. He said although I'd lived with primitive tribes before, this wasn't the Solomons or Irian Jaya, and that I could expect an indifferent reception from the clans living deep in the jungle. He warned me not to underestimate the island's harsh terrain, or its volatile inhabitants. The few trampers, tourists, and adventurers who trekked into the mountains normally followed the Jordan River and stuck to the lowlands.
Ni-Vanuatu are known for their cheerful natures and warm hospitality, but the highlanders, called man bush, were a different breed. They settled disputes with tribal warfare and would probably kill anyone who tried to photograph them.

Delving into the lives of isolated tribes that are separated from outsiders by dangerous geographical barriers, and by emotional barriers created by suspicion and prejudice, is always risky. John warned me again but needn't have bothered. It was obvious that the highlanders wouldn't hesitate to use violence against unwelcome visitors.

The next day, I was ecstatic when John found me a guide who wasn't afraid to walk across the island. He introduced me to Remmy, a small, moody, restless-looking man in his mid-twenties. We made an immediate start, and not long after sunset we entered Natchara, Remmy's home village. Throughout all of Vanuatu it's customary for a visitor to meet the chief. Remmy led me straight to his patriarch, a kind, aged man with warm eyes and a soft, broad smile. When I gave him a small bundle of *kava*[*] roots he reciprocated with a true mark of hospitality, by telling Remmy to welcome me with a *kava* drinking ceremony.

Kava is a bitter tasting, muddy looking brew, made with roots from the piper methysticum shrub. The word *kava* loosely translates to "intoxicating drink."

---

[*]On page 142 a glossary explains the meaning of the native words that are printed in italics.

Most evenings, men congregate in the *nakamal*, which is either a type of bar or a sacred men's hut used for drinking. In the more traditional areas a *nakamal* also houses *tabu* fetishes and objects that are used during worship.
Many Ni-Vanuatu believe *kava* creates a link to the supernatural. While they are under its influence they receive guidance, messages, and warnings from their ancestral spirits. If *kava* is taken in moderation it has medicinal properties, but when it's drunk in excess it causes impotence, lethargy, skin problems, and makes the eyes sensitive to sunlight. To refuse an offer to drink *kava* is to refuse friendship and is the ultimate insult to a host.
A *kava* ceremony is normally a vital part of important rituals or special occasions. The atmosphere is always solemn and respectful, and conversations are kept to a low murmur.

Before I came to Vanuatu I'd travelled around Fiji for four months and spent most nights drinking *kava* with the locals. If we had a big night and got drunk, the next morning I felt a bit tired and hung over, but apart from that I was fine. While Remmy gave me a warm welcome in the *nakamal*, I made a huge mistake by thinking Santo's *kava* would have the same effect. After my sixth cup I had double vision, the room started spinning violently, and the ground began to waver while my thoughts spiralled through different layers of my mind. The reason for everyone's previous look of awe became obvious when every cell in my body felt like it was slowing to a halt and turning to lead. I tried to move but my limbs were trapped in a nauseating world, where everything seemed surreal and my actions were in slow motion. I couldn't find my feet so I rolled around on the ground in a paralytic stupor until the heady brew sent me into a deep sleep.

When I woke up the next morning my mouth swung open before I'd even thought about prising my crusty eyes apart. I kept vomiting until I'd completely emptied my stomach, then I started bringing up a foul tasting yellow bile. While I gasped for air Remmy sounded excited when he said Linduri village was holding a *lafaet* and a three-day *kastom* dance that would make a great story.
I'd never felt so lethargic and hung over, and I doubted I'd be able to stay upright or walk properly, let alone make the 65-kilometre trek to Linduri. I stood up on my unsteady legs, noticed my hands were shaking uncontrollably, vomited again, and then staggered behind Remmy towards the main road.

Remmy had lied about knowing every trail that winds through the mountains and about being able to speak the highlander's languages, so when he insisted we needed three in our party for added safety, I agreed to hire another guide. He took me to a scruffy-looking villager whose skin was so badly affected by *kava* he looked twice as bad as I felt.

Wintae was a hardcore *kava* addict who looked about fifty years old. He whooped and laughed and slapped his leg in approval when Remmy introduced me and explained why I was throwing up again. I quickly accepted Wintae's offer to act as a guide. His patient-looking face, laid-back personality, and good sense of humour made him instantly likeable.

Wintae's kava ravaged feet.

Two days later I was still violently ill, and totally exhausted from pushing myself beyond what I thought were the limits of my endurance. I felt a huge sense of relief when just before dusk we crossed a wide expanse of boulders that had been washed down the mountains during a recent flash flood. Linduri was only minutes away and we'd made it in time for the start of the three-day *lafaet*.

As we entered the village a crowd of about one hundred people were listening to a stern warning from their chief. While he shouted that during the celebrations drinking or fighting wouldn't be tolerated I could see most of the youths had already ignored him. They were staggering around after getting drunk on *kava*, home brew, cheap wine, methylated spirits, and aftershave. A few of them had gotten high by boiling torch batteries and then drinking a vile-tasting cocktail made from the acidic dregs.

That night, when a swirling mass of energetic villagers danced for hours, they were a ticking time bomb. The inevitable happened when their emotions ran out of control and everyone's excited whoops and yells turned to angry screaming and pained cries when chaotic, full-on brawls erupted. Plenty of blood flowed and anyone within arm's reach was fair game.

The next morning, when I asked the superstitious locals about the pygmies, they spoke about three-foot-high beings who looked like devils, with long flowing beards, pointed teeth, and matted hair that draped to their ankles. Some of them said there were ferocious creatures living deep in the interior that ran around naked and had an insatiable appetite for human flesh. The Mentawai people I lived with in Indonesia chiselled their teeth to a point, and so do some of Africa's pygmies, so I didn't completely ignore the exaggerated descriptions.

Later in the day, when a twelve-foot aluminium dinghy rode the crest of a wave onto the beach, a cheerful European with a fat belly and smiling eyes jumped out and inspected his damaged boat. He was a scientist who'd travelled around Vanuatu for over thirty years measuring seismic activitiy. A large wave had creased the bow of his dinghy when he'd sailed from Malakula Island to take new readings on Santo. Our conversation quickly drifted to his experiences with remote tribes.

Years ago on Malakula, he'd feared for his life during frightening encounters with rarely visited clans, and although he'd never visited Santo's highlands, he'd heard numerous rumours that the inhabitants hated outsiders. I wasn't interested in taking timid footsteps along the coast and wondering about what lay hidden in the mountains, but I took serious heed of his warning to treat the region with extreme caution.

We had another night of wild and energetic dancing and although Wintae and Remmy had agreed to start our expedition first thing in the morning, we partied with the villagers into the small hours.

The next morning, when we learnt a cargo ship hadn't arrived to restock the tiny village store, it cast a grim shadow over our journey. There was nothing left for us to buy. Everything that we needed had been used during the *kastom* feast.

Our only food was a small packet of cabin biscuits that I'd bought in Luganville, and they'd been partially eaten by a rat.

To even consider travelling inland without any provisions was reckless, but Remmy felt confident we could live off the land and get food from another village, so we agreed to carry on. After an all-night drinking binge, Wintae would've blissfully snored the day away if we hadn't given him a good shake. He rubbed his bloodshot eyes, scratched his head, and then looked at our pitiful packet of biscuits when I said it was all we had. He muttered, "No problem," then said we should get moving as we had a hard day ahead of us.

After a small group of villagers gave us a handful of cooked vegetables and warned us about being eaten by the devils in the jungle, we started our journey by rock hopping up the boulder-strewn Vakola River. Wintae wore a cheap pair of jandals, but he still climbed over large greasy boulders with ease. We spent hour after hour leaping from boulder to boulder, which was much quicker and easier than trying to travel through the jungle. On each side of the river, sheer ridges covered in impenetrable rainforest ran down from a rugged mountainous

A pygmy with a wild dog he arrowed. The superstitious lowlanders believed the tiny highlanders were devils.

spine. The further we travelled inland, the happier Wintae became. If he wasn't whistling a happy tune he sang *kastom* songs at the top of his voice, and seemed to draw energy from some type of soulful connection he had with our beautiful surroundings.

For the next two days, we used Wintae's suspect navigation to travel through incredibly rugged terrain. After hours of pushing through thick jungle and making gruelling climbs up and down sheer ridges, he would look bewildered and apologetic, and then he calmly and matter-of-factly told us to retrace our steps.
When he did this a couple of times I decided travelling inland without adequate food was foolhardy enough, but to do it without knowing the way was suicidal. In country this rough, I needed a lot more than a map and a compass and a burning curiosity to keep me going. I used my only sensible option and headed down to the coast to try to find another guide at Naramach village.

We reached Naramach just as the setting sun disappeared into the horizon. Although I offered the destitute villagers tempting amounts of money, even the staunchest-looking men refused to guide me into the highlands. They all felt it was too dangerous. As a last resort, after a villager reluctantly gave us directions, Remmy and Wintae agreed to head inland again in the morning.

During the next few days, while we travelled through a maze of luscious rainforest, our lack of food and the gruelling terrain started to affect our health. We knocked wild pable-mous from the top of a tree with well-aimed sticks, but eating the juicy fruit didn't satisfy our lingering hunger. Just before midday, Wintae managed to find the base of a steep trail on the edge of the Jordan River. This time his internal compass had been right. The track led to the remote tribes living in the highlands.

Remmy and Wintae looked worried as they grappled for roots and firm handholds to slowly pull themselves up the almost vertical climb. John Noel had told me about a track that soared up from the Jordan River, and from his description I was pretty sure this was the same place.
During the famed Coconut Rebellion of 1980, Jimmy Stevens had tried to claim independence for Santo and wanted to reclaim all undeveloped land from the Europeans. This trail was where soldiers from Papua New Guinea had tried to mop up the last of Steven's rebellious followers. When the Papuans refused to start climbing it was just as well, because half way up, Steven's primitive supporters were hiding amongst the trees and ready to rain down a hail of arrows.

I learnt later that this natural barrier is also a spiritual blockade. Around 1970 a devastating earthquake killed every inhabitant of Vonumatui village, which had been perched at the top of the climb. Ever since the catastrophe, a mysterious bright light hovers above where the village used to be.

The superstitious highlanders are adamant that *Damate*, the spirit devil, destroyed Vonumatui and they refuse to go anywhere near the cliff. They call the rise Mount Lappemarau, and believe the eerie light is a devil. There are species of fireflies that swarm in large numbers and glow as a swirling mass, which could be responsible for the mystifying lights. The legend attached to the area, and knowing that any error in judgement during the climb would probably result in a serious injury, made Remmy and Wintae nervous.

Once we safely reached the top, after all of our minor setbacks we were finally heading through the jungle towards the heart of the island. We crossed a tangle of greasy roots along a razorback ridge, then when the roots gave way to mud, a cool steady drizzle turned the undulating track into a leech-infested quagmire. For the next six hours we put our faith in Wintae's unreliable navigation again while we blindly trekked through the mountains. By the end of the day his feet had become a split and bloodied mess, but his cheap jandals had managed to hold together.

A swathe of opaque cloud cloaking the numerous mountain ranges reduced the setting sun to a cold, insipid glow. Our search for a village had been futile, so in the remaining light we quickly set up a makeshift camp. We ate coconut flesh, had a pablemous each, and steamed bush cabbage inside a piece of bamboo, but it didn't stave off the hunger pangs stabbing at our grumbling stomachs. When we curled up on a bed of damp fern alongside a blazing fire, throughout the night we were shaken awake by the bitterly cold conditions of our crude, elevated camp.

Rick's primitive leaf hut. Nukurekum village.

The Stone Age Meets The Clone Age

When the rising sun cast light over the highlands and gave warmth to our cold bodies, the eye-catching views were the same in every direction. We were surrounded by an endless succession of sharp ridges and plunging valleys that resembled a mapmaker's nightmare. I felt comfortably cradled in a botanical paradise rather than captured by the island's unyielding geography, and although I was tired and hungry, I still thrived on every minute of our weary travel through the challenging landscape.

Late in the afternoon, Wintae climbed a tall tree, yodelled several times from up in the canopy, and patiently waited for a reply. Only his shrill echo answered. An hour later, our spirits soared when we intersected a well-used track. We slid down the steep trail and then climbed to the top of a ridge so that I could look for a village through my camera's telephoto lens. A huge smile spread across my face when away in the distance, on a grass-covered knoll, I saw faint wisps of smoke rising from two leaf huts.

As we trekked towards the tiny hamlet a bitter wind drove sheets of blinding rain in our faces. Then when the rain stopped a thick mist raced down the hillsides and engulfed us in a ghoulish fog. I could see Remmy and Wintae were nervous. They were probably afraid that *Damate* was responsible for the abrupt change in the weather.

I knew we were about to contact the remote highlanders, but I didn't realize just how far we were about to clamber back through the ages.

When I walked through a dense wall of mist and a withered old woman raised her head, it was like stepping into a surreal time warp. Her white nose bone matched the enlarged whites of her eyes and she shook from head to toe. After she screamed several times she threw her heavy load of taro to the ground and fled into the jungle as fast as her trembling legs could carry her.

Later, I discovered the poor woman's name was Vetrivu. She was over seventy years old, and had never travelled beyond her tribal boundaries or seen a white man.

This wasn't the first time I've been the only European a primitive person has seen. To be buzzing with awe, and to feel excitement in every fibre of my body while the natives are filled with rage or are quivering with fear, isn't easily forgotten. Those brief encounters have changed me forever. When I materialized from the mist like some sort of alien, it was literally a haunting experience for the terrified woman. To Vetrivu, I wasn't a human being made from flesh and blood. I was either *Damate*, who is normally jet black but can sometimes appear as a white spirit, or because the highlanders believe their spirit turns white when they die, I was an ancestral ghost.

An unnerving commotion muffled Vetrivu's fading screams. The sound of running feet frantically pounding the earth and blood-curdling shouts paved the way for five men armed with bows and machetes. When they came charging out of the mist it was our turn to experience a fear that can be so overwhelming it has to be experienced to be understood. The muscular warrior's menacing glares made it obvious that they hated the white man. In the past, during volatile situations with primitive people, I'd learnt revealing your true emotions is an unthinkable luxury. While Remmy gingerly moved forward and explained we were walking across the island, the barbed arrow that was aimed at my chest slowly lowered. Then the hostility suddenly changed to hospitality when Ravae, the village chief, spoke to Remmy in Bislama. We were welcome to stay in a nearby village, but only for one night. A strict tribal law demanded that I leave tomorrow at first light. I swore under my breath and quietly let out a massive sigh of relief while we followed the warriors down a ridge towards four large leaf huts.

Old women wearing nose bones trembled and screamed when we walked past their huts to a decrepit looking *nakamal*. The men wore *mul mul*s, and the bare-breasted women covered their crotches and the clefts of their buttocks with *nagria* leaves. Several naked toddlers who were hugging their shoulders to ward off the cold tearfully sprinted into their mother's shaking arms. Their scanty attire gave them little protection against the chilly weather, but these were a resilient people who had evolved to survive in the highland's changeable climate.

When Ravae led us inside the *nakamal* and a group of men and boys spilled into the hut, all of them were way too tall to be pygmies. While the *nakamal* hummed with quiet chatter, I answered questions that were asked in a harsh, abrupt manner. At first I thought everyone was being obnoxious, until Remmy said they normally spoke with an abrasive tone.

The beard Ravae wore, and his calm mannerisms, gave him the dignified look of a man who was at ease with himself and with others. He was the only one with a raised scar in the middle of his chest, but everyone had small circular scars on their upper arms and two vertical rows of scars on their stomachs. Some of the older villagers wore single lines of tattoos on their faces.

When eleven men crowded around me, their blend of curiosity and antagonism created an uncomfortable and unpredictable mood. To help them relax I passed around photos of myself living with other tribes. They were a great ice-breaker. Everyone was fascinated and in absolute awe that I'd spent months with peoples who still lived like they did.
They fingered the photos and whooped and yelled with excitement. But when a boy shouted "*Damate*!" when he saw a shot of me with a woman from Irian Jaya, it caused an uproar.
To someone with a primitive mindset she could easily be mistaken for a devil. It took a while to reassure everyone that the inhuman looking woman was really a withered mortal.
Once they calmed down they pawed at the photos again and noisily discussed the similarities between themselves and the tribes I'd visited. The shots I'd taken of pygmies in the Solomons generated a universal reaction. Everyone looked astonished, studied them carefully, and then said "winea."

Rick with an emaciated Yali woman from Irian Jaya that the villagers thought was a devil.

A hail of snot and spit rained around our feet when everyone got ready to chew *kava* for a welcome ceremony. After they'd cleared their airways they crammed their mouths full with *kava* chips, started chewing, and managed to carry on talking while they breathed through their noses.
Throughout Vanuatu *kava* is normally drunk on an empty stomach. The highlanders call this "letting the *kava* work." It makes them get intoxicated quicker, which creates a more powerful link with the supernatural. I knew this, but because I was starving I imitated someone eating. When Ravae handed me a cast iron pot about a dozen cockroaches that had been hiding beneath it scurried for cover.

I lifted the lid and cringed when a disgusting smell assaulted my senses. But hunger had sharpened my appetite, and dulled any doubts I had about committing hygiene suicide again. I reached in with my fingers and ate handfuls of rice and rotten beef.

Looking at the thick layers of green, yellow, and black plaque on everyone's teeth also made my stomach churn. The government has made chewing *kava* illegal, but in the remote regions this law is ignored. So is the risk of catching hepatitis, tuberculosis, and other fatal diseases from saliva and bleeding gums. I grabbed a handful of vile tasting *kava* chips and chewed until my lips went numb. While I added my pathetic looking mouthful to the growing pile of pulped root Remmy told everyone I'd drunk six cups of strong *kava* at Natchara. Either my sheer stupidity or my amazing drinking ability spread a smile across everyone's faces. The chief always drinks first, and after Ravae gulped down a shell (a cup made from coconut shell), anyone standing near or walking past stooped over like a question mark to show him respect. When he handed me a drink I downed it in one hit. Although *kastom* demanded we leave in the morning, we'd just performed a vital ritual. This important part of protocol sealed our temporary friendship.

Whenever I looked at Ravae, his eyes were riveted on my every move. I could almost feel his intense gaze burning into the very core of my soul. Then he became silent and withdrawn, when shell after shell of the enlightening brew opened up his mind and created a portal to the supernatural. Half an hour later, after he'd been staring blankly at the ground, he suddenly snapped out of his trance and sat upright. Everyone fell silent when he said the ancestral spirits had told him that I wasn't a white man, I was the reincarnation of his dead grandfather's spirit. When he said my real name was *Tavua*, (Ta means man, vua from the jungle), everyone acknowledged his startling announcement by saying my name over and over. I was stunned.

The isolated hamlet felt anything but remote when Ravae added it had just become my new home. Everyone's attitude suddenly changed. Their reluctance to make any kind of physical contact was gone, and for the first time, the fascinated villagers explored the body of a *disale*. While their inquisitive hands started feeling the texture of my hair, fondled my chest, stroked my skin, and squeezed my athletic body, they said, "*Tamamasa Tavua. Tamamasa Tavua*" ("Everything is good Tavua. Everything is good Tavua"). Ravae seemed pleased with himself when he stood up, said goodnight, and disappeared into the darkness with everyone following behind him.

A leech bite on my ankle had become badly infected when we waded through mud and stagnant pools. I'd taken antibiotics, but it had turned septic so quickly that pus oozed from a

gaping hole I was dressing in the firelight. I felt exhausted, elated, and extremely privileged as I stretched out on a woven sleeping mat laid over a thin layer of *lap lap* leaves.
While the men sang and danced to the beat of throbbing *tam tams* and *bolos* in a nearby hut, I slipped into a deep blissful sleep. During the night I was too comatose from the *kava* to feel the insects feeding on the remnants of food on my unwashed hands and lips.

The next morning, parts of my skin were so red and tender I avoided touching them, and my throbbing thumb looked like a huge welt. I was glad that the rats living in the rafters didn't chew on my food-scented flesh, as I've seen the horribly mutilated face of a child who was eaten alive in a rat-infested hut. Forgetting to wash after I'd eaten was careless, but my mind had whirled from the *kava* and from the dramatic announcement Ravae made. Due to the actions of the devious white men who first visited Vanuatu, throughout the highlands Europeans are associated with death, disease, disrespect, and deception. To have gained any type of acceptance from an uncompromising people who thought I was a devil, a ghost, or a hated *disale* was incredible.

Peta pounding out a tune with bolo sticks.

When I rolled off my sleeping mat and stepped outside a man in his mid-twenties was patiently waiting for me. He had a soft melodious voice, a powerful build, and friendly mannerisms.
As he gave me a roasted taro he said, "Here breakfast Tavua. My name Gramma." His English was hardly perfect, but it came as an unexpected and welcome surprise. Especially when I learnt he'd grasped the basics from a friend while he spent several months in Luganville.

Gramma used broken English and Bislama to explain that this village was called Vanakanakarea and used the same language and customs as Winea, Porea, Nukurekum, Matai Lono, Vunasuli, Tapuimoli, and Vavoru.

Most of the books I'd read about the colonials making contact with the natives have a saddening history of the exploiters and the exploited. This is why the highlanders hate the white man. If a visitor is lucky, he can stay for one night, but most of the few outsiders who have entered Middle Bush (the highlands) were forced to leave immediately.

I wasn't the first European to stay at Vanakanakarea. An adventurous missionary had spent one night there, but his refusal to drink *kava* and accept the local food was a huge insult. He was threatened with violence and told to leave. Ni-Vanuatu are welcome if they ask absolutely nothing about *kastom*. Any visitor who causes problems is beaten to a bloody pulp and then physically thrown from the village. If a guest commits a severe enough breach of *kastom* he is killed.

Gramma

After our wild reception, I wasn't surprised to learn that the highlanders were in the middle of a tribal war. Some of the coastal villages at Matantas have been their traditional enemy for centuries. A few of them have moved inland and had recently stolen the highlanders *kava*, planted on land they own down in the lowlands. It was because of an already tense atmosphere that we'd been greeted with drawn bows.

Some of highlanders are so reclusive they've never seen the world beyond their tribal boundaries. Gramma guessed at least half the villagers have visited Luganville to sell *kava*, purchase rice and other luxuries, or simply to satisfy their curiosity.

I later befriended Tutino, a man in his mid-twenties, who'd been to town four times. The first time he saw tourists in the main street he trembled with fear and was convinced that seeing so many *Damates* together signalled the end of the world. Despite his apprehension, he always greeted me with a wide smile. As our friendship grew stronger, even after I carefully explained why our skin tones were different, his absolute belief in *kastom* made him sure I was a *Damate* or an ancestral ghost in disguise.

Gramma explained that the highlanders' complex religion isn't a separate part of everyday life, as it can be with other beliefs. *Kastom* includes every aspect of the natural and supernatural worlds. He warned me to be extremely careful, because even asking about *kastom* can be fatal. The villagers would think I was trying to steal their culture. Under tribal law, the penalty to both a careless informant and the recipient of sacred customs is death. If the ancestral spirits approve, closely guarded knowledge can be shared with others, but only if it's reciprocated with a gift and if the informant is positive the people's well-being isn't at risk. By the end of the day Gramma and I had become good friends, and over the next ten years our friendship would save my life numerous times.

That evening, as a heavy mist started to sag over the ranges, Ravae returned to the village caked in mud and lathered in sweat. He'd visited hundreds of ancestral skulls hidden in a sacred cave deep in the jungle. After chanting to the bones for hours, he chewed *tabu* leaves and drank *tabu kava* to create a link with the spirit world. Then he carried a *tabu* banana plant back from the sacred site, and in the last of the fading light I planted it alongside the *nakamal*.

This simple ritual, called the *essengo*, formed a bond as strong as brotherhood. Ravae knew I had to return to New Zealand. While I was away, he would weed the plant and nurture its growth. Then when I returned, I'd eat the first fruit it produced, we'd perform a *kava* ceremony together, and I'd finish the rite by giving him either a pig, a fowl, or a woven mat. Whenever Ravae walked past the plant he would have heart-warming thoughts about Tavua, his beloved *kastom* brother.

I couldn't ask anything about the consequences of the *essengo* until it was over. If I didn't return before a year had passed to complete the rite the outcome would be terrible. The next time Ravae saw me he'd shoot me with his bow or attack me with another weapon. *Kastom* demanded at the very least my blood must flow and my bones must break. If I retaliated I'd be killed, and even if I did manage to survive I faced eternal banishment. What was left of me would be carried to the edge of the village and thrown in the jungle to fend for myself. But if I successfully reciprocated the *essengo*, the bond between us would be so close, if we ever entered a battle we would willingly sacrifice our lives to save each other.

By performing the *essengo* I'd unwittingly become part of a ruthless society whose people were impossible to predict and even harder to understand. Although it's far easier for a native to think like the white man than it is for a *disale* to think like a man bush, they made it clear that if I breached a tribal law simply because I was unaware of their beliefs, *kastom* allowed no room for compromise, and if the circumstances demanded it I'd be killed.

I'd entered a timeless world, where being violent and manipulating the spirits is considered normal. Neither believing nor disbelieving in God and being born and conditioned to live in a modern society made it extremely difficult for me to understand the highlanders' belief in *kastom* and the supernatural.

The next day, when Ravae offered me a full initiation into his clan I was stunned and honoured. This was a once-in-a-lifetime opportunity to learn about human nature from an untouched primitive people. An outsider had never been given an insight into their brutal culture. I knew it would be dangerous and I'd have to compromise my morals and beliefs, but I took the plunge and became a member of the highlanders' fascinating society.

Over the next few days, I spent each evening in the *nakamal*, taking notes and hanging on Ravae and Gramma's every word as they shared millennia of history and local customs. *Kastom* limited the amount of information they could give me. It wasn't until I'd completed my initiation that I'd fully appreciate the implications of becoming a member of the tribe. For an illiterate people whose history is passed on by word of mouth, they recalled events that occurred centuries ago with vividness, passion, and incredible ease.

The seeds of mistrust were planted in the highlands when the Spanish explorer, Pedro Ferdinand de Quiros, discovered Espiritu Santo in 1606. From the moment the Spaniards set foot on the island they faced numerous dangers. After enduring months of hardship at sea the travel-weary sailors suffered from fish poisoning, caught malaria, and fought bloody battles with the natives. One bloodthirsty crew member shot a villager, cut off his head and foot, and then hung the mutilated body in a tree. This enraged the chiefs, and as a consequence, the fighting became so intense the disgruntled and diseased Spaniards abandoned the island.

Then came the whalers, whose visits to the islands usually caused chaos and bloodshed. Blackbirders followed to steal the natives' bodies, and then the missionaries came for their souls. Finally the colonists arrived to take their lands. It was the devious blackbirders who created the highlander's initial hatred of Europeans. While they recruited their human merchandise from Santo, they anchored their slave ships offshore and ignited sticks of dynamite. When the explosions reverberated off the mountain ranges and rolled down the valleys some of the natives walked for days to satisfy their curiosity. Many of them were either tricked into visiting the ship or were forced on board by gunpoint. Then they were shipped abroad to work in the sugarcane fields in Queensland at Australia or at Fiji, where the work was cruel and the hours were long for ridiculously small wages. The unsanitary and inhuman living conditions on the blackbirding ships and at the plantations led to high mortality rates. Once the islanders became wise to the atrocities they greeted returning ships with violence.

The highlanders are a naturally violent peoples.

Sometimes the natives worked for years to get an axe or a rifle, which proved to be a poisoned form of payment. Before guns were introduced, warring tribes had merely irritated each other with their bows and other primitive weapons. When they killed the enemy with simple weapons during payback disputes, only enough blood was spilled to please the ancestral spirits. Arming tribes with rifles resulted in bloody massacres, but by far the most deadly and despicable thing the Europeans ever did was purposely introducing microbes, by returning infected natives to their villages as retribution for previous attacks on the blackbirders. Because the Ni-Vanuatu didn't have any immunity to the introduced diseases, the fatal epidemics led to rapid depopulation throughout the island.

The only advantage that came from blackbirding was the introduction of new crops. Plantation owners carefully searched the slaves returning to Vanuatu so that they didn't take any seeds back, but a native hid corn seeds in his rectum when he left Australia, and another smuggled tarovit (Fijian taro) from Fiji.

Fanatical missionaries with questionable motives worsened the highlander's prejudice towards the white man. The biggest barrier between trying to integrate societies that have conflicting religions is a lack of understanding or failing to have an appreciation of each other's outlook on life. The highlanders weren't going to compromise their beliefs, especially for a white-skinned devil. Any evangelist who was foolish enough to enter Middle Bush was guaranteed a swift death.

The last cannibal feast with a missionary on the menu occurred in the early 1960s, at Hapuna, near the base of Mount Tambewessana. The reckless preacher was killed the instant he set foot in the village. Everyone enjoyed the non-smoking, clean-living Christian's untainted meat, except for those who ate his leathery feet. Some of the naïve cannibals with aching jaws and indigestion thought his boots were part of his anatomy.

Like the other white men who'd invaded the natives' lives, I also hoped to gain something from them. I sought their hidden truths, but not by using educated lying or shrewd deception. From what Gramma and Ravae had told me, if I wanted to safely document their beliefs, I needed endless amounts of patience.

Theft, black magic, land disputes, breaching tribal law, and adultery are the main causes of conflict in Middle Bush. Each night, ten men joined us in the *nakamal* to drink *kava* and plan an attack on the men from Matantas that had been stealing our *kava* down in the lowlands. Now that I'd performed the *essengo*, *kastom* demanded that I fight to the death against our enemies. During my youth I'd studied several martial arts, but I absolutely hate any kind of violence. Courage and the ability to fight are admired traits in the highlands, so if I wanted to gain total acceptance the fight was also mine.

When I'd decided to become a man bush the morals I had in Western society ceased to exist, so I made it known that I wouldn't hesitate to kill an enemy. When I told Ravae my badly infected ankle required immediate treatment, and he saw the puss-filled mess, he knew I wasn't being a coward and agreed that if I chose to use modern medicines I should leave for Luganville in the morning.

The next morning, it only took me five minutes to hike from Vanakanakarea to the village I was going to live in when I returned. Nukurekum had six tidy-looking huts, and when I quietly looked inside the doorway of my new home, once my eyes adjusted to the gloomy light, I could see poor Vetrivu cringing in a corner, shaking from head to toe. I was amazed that for an island this size the only modern items I could see were a few old bottles filled with salt, pots, axes, machetes, a couple of plastic bowls, and a rusty kerosene lamp. The odd pair of jandals, brightly coloured bead necklaces, and several watches worn by natives who couldn't tell the time didn't really taint the primitive atmosphere.

When Gramma introduced me to his middle-aged mother, Voemanu, she looked photogenic with her solid physique, short greying hair, tattooed face, and shell nose bone. Her infectious smile and wicked sense of humour made her instantly likeable. She smirked at me and said, "*Himi frite*," ("she's afraid") then she reassured her mother, Vetrivu, that I wasn't dangerous and meant her no harm.

When Voemanu agreed to let me take her photo, her husband, Peta, the second most powerful *kastom* man in the highlands, also stood in the shot. From the instant I laid eyes on him, I knew I'd have to tread carefully. His hatred of the white man was blatant, and he had zero tolerance for even the slightest breach of *kastom*. But beneath his rugged exterior he also had a kind heart and caring nature.

I tried to explain how photography worked, but when I pointed the camera at Voemanu she seemed frightened and uncertain of what was about to happen. She screamed "Wiiii!" and then ran behind the hut. Because some of the others burst out laughing, I jokingly started running on the spot, to make out I was going to chase her. Without any warning, Peta nocked an arrow to his bow and began screaming abuse in my face. I could tell from the burning look of hatred in his eyes that the threat was very real.

Gramma said something to him in his native tongue that defused the tense situation, and then he took me aside and said I'd come within a gnat's whisker of being shot. He calmly warned that if I ever treated anyone with disrespect or upset his mother again he wouldn't hesitate to help Peta kill me.

The last thing I'd wanted was to offend Peta and Voemanu, so I quickly offered them a sincere apology.

It was disappointing to have made such a bad first impression, because when I returned and shared their hut they were going to be my *kastom* parents.

Before I left with Remmy and Wintae, Ravae gave me a woven mat to signify we were true *kastom* brothers and promised to name his next-born son Tavua.

Physically, the mat was mine, but spiritually it belonged to *yumi* (you and me) and symbolized that we shared an inseparable bond.

Ricks *kastom* mother, Voemanu, weaving a mat.

It was a huge honour, so I reciprocated by giving him a bracelet that was a gift from a Mentawai shaman, which was the only thing I had that I really cherished.

We said goodbye, then while we walked along a trail heading down to the lowlands, the sound of the villagers singing a heartfelt farewell and shouting out my name was a magical and deeply moving experience.
I didn't want to leave. When I'd asked Ravae about the whereabouts of the legendary pygmy tribe he'd smiled and replied, "When you come next year, Tavua."
After we crossed the island I felt a real sense of achievement, but then I put things into perspective by thinking that our adventurous journey was what the highlanders do during everyday life.

The day after we left, Ravae and ten warriors went to the Lappe River to kill the lowlanders who'd been stealing their *kava*. When they found them, forty armed men from Navale village were standing on the opposite bank, primed for a fight. Because the highlanders were grossly outnumbered and the lowlanders had rifles, Gramma's quick thinking abruptly ended what probably would have been a massacre. Two rifle shots drowned out the flurry of taunts and screams of abuse, and three poorly aimed arrows hissed harmlessly through the air before he threw a rock at Navele's paramount chief. The wounded chief dropped like a stone. While blood pumped down his face from a gaping hole in his temple, his shocked warriors made a hasty retreat and carried his unconscious body back to their village.
The seriously wounded chief eventually made a full recovery, then a few months later, after he paid the highlanders compensation, a *kava* ceremony temporarily healed the rift between the two tribes.

Ancestral skulls are used to connect with the supernatural.

Crossing The Cultural Divide

While I was in New Zealand and getting ready to head back to Vanuatu, I knew I was about to unravel the mystery surrounding the pygmies' existence. It made my decision to return to the hostilities and fascination of Middle Bush society surprisingly easy. Knowing that I was about to live an explorer's dream come true was exhilarating, but what really excited me was returning to a primitive culture that still enjoyed a freedom other persecuted tribes have lost forever.

When I arrived in Vanuatu it felt like my second home. Luganville had the look and feel of a frontier town, and hardly gleamed with beauty, but it was a comfortable place to return to. While I walked past the unkempt buildings that line the main street I ran into Garae, a staunch-looking thirty-year-old *kastom* man from Vanakanakarea. The massive loads of firewood he carried nearly everyday had transformed his shoulders into calloused chords of thick muscle, and his bull neck was way out of proportion to the rest of his lithe body. He was selling *kava* and invited me to head back to Middle Bush with him in the afternoon. We headed inland for three hours on the back of a pickup that bounced over badly rutted roads, then we walked through the jungle until dusk and spent the night at Malories village.

The next morning, while the first shards of light crept over the horizon, Garae led us to the edge of the Jordan River. When I saw a native sitting on a rock downstream, from a distance the silhouette of his well-developed body made him look huge. But as we drew closer and his dimensions gained perspective, he kept getting smaller. I was bursting with excitement, but divorced myself from expressing any emotion when Garae pointed to a pygmy patiently waiting for us on the riverbank.

The little pygmy didn't look anything like the legendary devils that terrified the superstitious natives. Busa wore a short beard, had tightly cropped hair, and was less than four feet nine inches tall, which is the maximum height of a true pygmy. His tiny Herculean frame, his dignified mannerisms, and the noble look on his face captivated me. I didn't realise it at the time, but the patriarch of the legendary pygmy tribe was standing in front of me. He'd also become the paramount chief for the highlands, by rearing and slaughtering sacrificial fowl and pigs. Garae had simply said that Busa was to be treated with the utmost respect. That couldn't have been any easier.

After I introduced myself, Busa said in a blunt tone that although I was a reincarnation I was still physically a white man, and if I broke any customs or showed the slightest bit of disrespect I would be punished with a brutal tribal law. From the harsh look in his eyes he obviously meant every word when he mimicked with his machete how he would cut off my testicles and penis. Then after he'd forced me to eat my own genitals, he'd shoot me with his bow, cook my body in hot stones, and cannibalise me.

Garae, preparing a kava stalk for planting.

Mother Nature was in a fickle mood when we started heading inland. Up in the mountains, Vanuatu's highest peaks where covered by dark sheets of torrential rain that had sluiced down the valleys and turned the Jordan River into a violent surge of white water. To attempt the river crossings would've been suicidal, so we made a wide detour and I entered the highlands through virgin territory. When we reached a massive boulder with a groove in it, Busa pointed at it and said, "Tavua you climb to the top and piss." While Garae solemnly agreed by nodding his head, the thought of Busa's machete leaving me nothing to piss out of if I refused sent me scurrying up the boulder. I hoped my audience wouldn't give me stage fright, and after a bit of grunting I forced myself to urinate down the groove to chase away *Pulminero*, the spirit devil.

Thousands of years ago, *Pulminero* had pulled the massive boulder to the top of a mountain with a *kastom* rope made from pandanus leaves. When the ancestral spirits saw what he was doing, they snapped the rope and the massive rock crashed back down to the riverbed. Ever since then, anyone passing through the area for the first time must urinate on the boulder to stop *Pulminero* killing them by rolling huge rocks down the hillsides.

I received a warm greeting at Nukurekum. Several older women were still afraid of my white skin, but once they got over the initial shock of seeing a *disale* again they were as receptive as the other villagers. A small girl who was bent over double and clutching her stomach to ease her pain was a grim reminder of how brutal life is in Middle Bush. The highlanders are affectionate towards their children, but they won't tolerate a lack of discipline. Her father had whipped her with a stick until blood flowed, and when that didn't control her rebellious attitude he made numerous cuts across her stomach with a bamboo knife.

Most of the time Busa controlled his people in a more humane way. I noticed he was sociable and cheerful while he spoke to the villagers. While I renewed my friendship with Gramma, he said Busa was always considerate, was loved by everyone, and was more than just a mortal and a respected leader. His special relationship with the spirits and his vast knowledge of *kastom* made him a demigod. Before he left Nukurekum to head deeper into the mountains to his village, he made another threat to cut off my penis and eat me if I breached *kastom*. I didn't ask Busa about his clan. Being patient and having a deep understanding of the people's social behaviour was vital if I wanted to survive living in other villages.

Gramma started sharing *kastom* with me straight away. He knew that if I wanted to stay alive I had to carefully reach the top of my steep learning curve as quickly as possible. The first thing I learnt was our hut is also Nukurekum's *nakamal*. Fortunately the sixteen metres long by seven metres wide dwelling had plenty of room for me to distance myself from Vetrivu. She hadn't overcome her fear of living with a white devil and was so terrified she cringed in a dark corner and refused to look at me.

Everyone in Middle Bush lives as a huge extended family. Communal living and socializing are extremely important. A man bush who lives alone or is unhappy is seen to be inadequate. To be complete he must communicate well with others and "*hearem gud*" (feel good) so that everyone feels contented. Gramma warned that anyone who was miserable couldn't be trusted and would never be in sync with all of nature, which meant they could never enjoy a good relationship with the spirits and the *kastom* god.

We had four permanent residents in our hut, including myself. Over the next few days a steady stream of friends and relatives visited to gossip, share meals, and check out the *disale*. I'd often wake up in the middle of the night and find a total stranger sitting at the end of my sleeping mat, quietly staring at the white man bush novelty.

Rick with Busa, the cannibalistic pygmy chief.

Nukurekum felt like home and our hut provided me with basic comforts, but whenever Ravae and Gramma shared *kastom* with me, out of necessity I memorized everything over and over, as if I was studying for an exam. There was so much crucial information to remember. Until I knew every *tabu*, moving around our hut was like walking through a minefield.

If I mistakenly used the women's entrance, slept on a brother's mat, used his wooden stool, walked past a sister the wrong way if I'd grown a beard, sat on her sleeping mat, or entered or left a hut during a healing ritual, it could result in severe punishment. If the circumstances demand it, the fine of a fowl, a mat, or a pig is increased to a death sentence. It was so confusing, as some of the *tabus* blatantly contradicted the ethic of being selfless. I constantly kept my wits about me, and asked if I had the slightest doubt about breaching a *tabu*.

Our hut was a typical strong and functional highland dwelling. The walls are made from split bamboo, the thatch roof is built from sago palm leaves that keep out the strongest rain, and decades of human traffic have compacted the mud floor so that it feels as firm as concrete. Both sexes can move around the entire inside of a hut, but women can only sleep in the rear and males must enter and exit through the front door, which is low and narrow so that only one man can pass through.

This *tabu* originated thousands of years ago, when cannibalism and warfare were rampant and a chief named Kasus cast a spell that killed any male who entered the rear of a hut. Since then, the enemy always comes through the front door in single file. This gives the occupants a chance to defend themselves and helps to prevent an entire clan from being slaughtered.

I was incredibly lucky to be living with the most powerful and knowledgeable people in all of the highlands. Peta and Busa have the same potent supernatural powers and had passed all of their *tabu* wisdom on to Gramma. Busa is the spiritual father of every highlander, but he was especially fond of Gramma. He treated him like his own son and if anything important needed to be discussed he always sought and valued Gramma's opinion. I was also lucky to have performed the *essengo* with Ravae. He's one of the most feared and respected *kastom* men in Middle Bush.

There was so much to learn while the timeless days quickly slipped by and blended into timeless weeks. Whenever Gramma and Ravae taught me *kastom* I never asked any questions. I figured by quietly listening I'd gain more respect and would be given a much deeper insight into what I was trying to understand. My unusual approach worked.

One night, after they said we were in for a lengthy session, this is the exact order of the steady stream of customs and *tabus* that they shared with me. I've done this to give you an idea of what it was like trying to remember everything. Only a chief has rank. *Kastom* men are respected, but all the other men are treated as equals. If something is stolen a member of your own clan has never taken it. Another native, *Damate*, or black magic is responsible.

All females are inferior and they must always be spoken to in an assertive tone. A husband must never show his wife any physical affection in public. To kiss, hold hands, or hug a spouse is unthinkable, but a father can hug his daughter while she's still a child. Beating a wife or daughter is acceptable and expected, so long as blood is never drawn. If blood flows the offender stands before his chief and is fined a fowl, a mat, or a pig. If a woman with a "*strong head*" ("rude attitude") was disrespectful, I was to hit her without hesitation or I'd lose face with the men. Women have such a low social standing they don't have any special areas to perform *kastom*. They carry out their rituals wherever it's felt appropriate, and under a veil of secrecy, as men are forbidden to know about or watch women's *kastom*.

It was a huge relief when Ravae mentioned homosexuality is despised and anyone caught in a same sex relationship would be beaten to a bloody pulp.

After I'd completed my initiation, he wanted me to get married so that I could continue my bloodline. Pigs, money, and gifts are used as bride price. I needed to buy or raise ten pigs, or I could pay for my wife with eighty thousand vatu. The dowry is given to the bride's parents as a social rather than an economic transaction, and although females are held in low esteem, the bride price shows everyone that the groom recognises and appreciates his wife's womanhood. If the groom has an unwed sister, and the bride has a single brother, they must also marry to strengthen the bond between the two families.

Gramma didn't have any pigs or money when he chose his wife, so he gave his first-born girl to his wife's parents when she was three years old. The child can never return to see its parents, but they can visit their daughter at the grandparents' village.

When Gramma's daughter was given to her grandparents they put her to work immediately. Gramma and his wife were devastated. They cried for one full week, which is how long the parents must express their grief.

An only son who doesn't have bride price can marry a girl from another village by selling himself to her clan, so he increases their manpower. This very rarely happens, because although his family and friends can visit him and his wife, he's banished from his own village for life.

Gramma frowned and lowered his voice when he warned me that talking about sex in front of females is *tabu*. During sex a wife is only ever penetrated in the missionary position. If any other position is used it's believed she will never become pregnant.

A couple must always keep their eyes closed, as seeing the fully developed genitals of the opposite sex is strictly forbidden. None of the men knew what foreplay was or that a woman could have an orgasm. Intercourse is *tabu* while a woman is pregnant, so she keeps her husband satisfied by giving him oral sex. Any type of sex is forbidden out of wedlock. Anyone who breaks this *kastom* either suffers broken and bloodied limbs, has their genitals severed, is hacked up with a bush knife, shot with a bow, or stoned or clubbed to death. These brutal penalties ensure that overpopulation doesn't become a problem.

After a child is born, intercourse is *tabu* for the next three years, to give the infant the full benefit of its mother's milk.

I often saw five-year-old children sucking their mother's breast. This also helps to increase the infant's chances of survival, as the highlands have a high child mortality rate. Once a man has enough children he can simply abstain from sex, or his wife becomes sterile by chewing a leaf. Man bush has an intimate knowledge of the medicinal plants growing in the jungle, but hasn't found a leaf that makes men infertile.

Gramma told me things that were important in the outside world have little or no significance in Middle Bush, and that I'd have to learn a new set of priorities and the order of their value. Having an absolute belief in *kastom* is the ultimate because it includes everything in the natural and supernatural worlds. A garden provides food for friends and family and has the same importance as land. They are both an extension of our spiritual and physical being.

Water is vital to all of life. A hut provides shelter from the elements, enemies, and evil spirits. Pigs are used to buy a wife, to become a chief, for rituals, and to pay fines. A wife produces children and works hard in the garden. In her spare time she makes mats that are slept on, are used during rituals, and are used as currency. Children are the future and will pass on *kastom* to the next generation. Mats have various uses and provide comfort when they're slept on. Fowl are a food source and are also used for sacrifice and as payment for fines. *Kava* is last on the list of life's priorities. A man who doesn't plant *kava* is incomplete because the brew is an important ingredient during rituals and when the community socializes.

Ravae and Gramma spoke in a solemn tone to emphasize the importance of being respectful. Any visitors who are welcomed into the village must be treated with kindness and respect. Even during times of hardship, when we have little food, the needs of others must selflessly come before our own. They must be given the very best of what we have and treated as a loved brother or sister. Even a despicable *disale* must receive generous treatment until he leaves us.

Anyone who disrespects our hospitality or *kastom* must be beaten or, if need be, killed without hesitation. If I failed to attack them I would receive the same bloody punishment. We must always stand together and show our respect to *Taute* and the ancestral spirits by giving them instant revenge against an enemy or anyone who's disrespectful. The hospitality we so readily provided could suddenly turn into savage hostility.

The spirit of *Taute* is in everything, so I must respect all of nature. If I didn't strive to have a harmonious relationship with *Taute* and the entire universe, he wouldn't provide for me from nature's fruitful bounty, and I'd be unhappy and face a difficult future filled with constant turmoil. To keep my body, soul, and spirit healthy, I must constantly respect *Taute* and *kastom* so that he will help protect me from *Damate* and the evil spirits.

Man bush has an inseparable bond with all of nature.

The remains of our ancestors that are buried in the earth give us an eternal connection with the land and nature. Their spirits help our crops grow and also nurture our wellbeing while we live in their timeless world. We own our tribal land and have an inseparable bond with it, but while we are mortals we are only its temporary guardians, and we must always fight to the death to protect it.

Ravae became reverent and poetic when he said, "The cool refreshing breeze that drifts up the mountains and whispers to the leaves, the shimmering waters of the fish-filled rivers, the warming rays of the rising sun that cast growth throughout the land, and the soothing sounds of the rainforest are all sacred in the minds of man bush. We can never sell the land that beats in tune with our hearts. It would be like selling ourselves."
While I carefully listened to his every word, he asked, "Tavua, why does the white man spoil the land?" I answered, "There are many greedy *disale* who don't love the earth as a brother. They have no respect, and they treat nature as an enemy they need to conquer and control. Sometimes the *disale* treats other men the same."

Then Ravae said, "Tavua, when I go to Luganville, I see the *disale* is wise. He makes trucks, radios, and aeroplanes. Things man bush can't understand. The more I see the less I like. Luganville is too busy. It makes my head spin and my body slack. Tavua, the more our people learn from the wise *disale*, the more stupid we will become."

Ravae didn't hesitate to complain about the outside world, but moaning about anything that's related to *kastom* or life in Middle Bush is *tabu*. Man bush believes that complaint injures the soul. I must never moan about anything, even if I was in agony or violently ill. Showing any signs of weakness shames your clan, and worst of all, makes you vulnerable to an attack from the evil spirits and *Damate*.

Voemanu making salt from black palm ash.

The highlanders live in a mystical world where inexplicable powers are tangible and accepted as being real. Black magic is epidemic and creates constant havoc in a society that is far from perfect. Every death and every type of sickness is caused by black magic. The villagers know that mosquitoes carry malaria and bacteria cause sickness, but they believe evil spirits make the insects and microbes target victims who die or become diseased.

Although the highlanders are absolutely selfless, they are by far the most jealous-natured people I've met anywhere in the world. Anyone that prospers is attacked with a dangerous magic spell. Being a *disale* with costly boots, an expensive looking backpack, and other desirable Western goods made me extremely vulnerable.

If I visited other villages, finishing the last scrap of food from my plate was vital. This would prevent the leftovers from being used to cast a spell that could bring me bad luck, sickness, or even kill me. No one could be trusted. Even my best friend could be my worst enemy. Anyone from a village with the same *kastom* or a traditional enemy with different beliefs could use black magic against me. If I survived a physical assault, then spiritual warfare would also be used to help settle the score. Nothing is safe from an attack. Even a garden with poor crops has been hexed by a rival's spell.

I had to be wary of humans, but devils and powerful *kastom* men can also become embodied in the flesh of animals.

Dogs are the most feared, and a cat, a nighthawk (owl), and a fowl are dangerous as well. When a nighthawk flies over a hut and its ghoulish call is heard, it's *tabu* to leave the hut until daylight. If anyone needs to go to the toilet they use the corner of the hut. The nighthawk's lethal spirit kills those who are foolish enough to go outside. I thrived on having my brain overloaded with huge amounts of precious information, but as I left the *nakamal*, Gramma and Ravae said I still knew nothing and had a lot to learn.

While the days passed, and my head was being crammed full of complex *kastom*, it was difficult having to literally live off my wits by carefully watching everyone's actions. I enjoyed the practical side of the learning curve the most, when I was taught how to reap our goldmine of natural resources. While we used a primitive bow to shoot birds, fish, and a small pig, I silently crept through the jungle and learnt to move with the land instead of just passing through it.

The highlanders raise small numbers of domesticated pigs, cattle, and chickens and rely heavily on horticulture for their food. Although a wide variety of vegetables are grown, taro is the staple part of their diet. We gathered nuts and edible plants from the rainforest, speared eels in the rivers, and made salt from black palm ash. I was taught how to enjoy a rich and simple existence by using the most basic of implements. I loved the sense of freedom I felt from living off the land, but I didn't have any responsibilities and faced none of the pressures a subsistence lifestyle places on the villagers. Life in the mountains is hardly carefree; it requires a disciplined work ethic to grow enough crops and gather food from the jungle.

Early one morning, without giving me any warning Ravae entered our hut and said it was time for my initiation. I followed him up to Vanakanakarea's *nakamal* without saying a word. I knew I'd gain more respect by simply submitting to whatever was expected of me. While I shed my clothes, I also discarded my Western mindset, and when I tied a *mul mul* in place with a sacred *navola* vine, I decided to expose the whole of my being to the rite.

A group of curious men that had come from other villages, watched while Gramma and Ravae anointed my body with streaks of bright orange pigment from the *ol* nut and with *vavara*, a black paste made from ground charcoal mixed with saliva. While Ravae painted me he said he used the black mixture so *Taute* would see that although I'd been born with despicable *disale* skin, I still had the same blood and spirit of a true man bush. Everyone stood back when he put a laurel of *tabu mele mele* leaves on my head, and tied them around my biceps. They are so sacred only a chief can touch them. Then he tied a string of the *tabu* leaves around my neck, so the ancestral spirits and *Taute* would give me two spiritual bodyguards to constantly protect me, even when I left Middle Bush.

A hallowed hush, the type that showed this ritual demanded immense respect, cast a deadly quiet over the *nakamal* when Ravae gave me a large coconut shell filled with *kava*. The root that he'd chewed is so strong it's only ever used during *tabu* ceremonies.
This time I swapped cultures as well as saliva when I knocked back the foul-tasting brew in one hit. It coursed through my veins and made my senses reel while I watched the rest of the men drink a shell of the intoxicating brew. Torrential rain and tribal law had forced the women to shelter under the eaves outside the *nakamal*. It's *tabu* for them to see a male initiate being prepared. When the men were fully satisfied with my physical transformation the women were called inside. If it hadn't been raining, the rest of the ritual would've been held outside on the *nasara* (dance ground).

Ravae beating out a tune on the tam tam.

Ravae stood in the middle of the *nakamal* and started beating out a tune on a bamboo *tam tam*. While he looked to the heavens and sang a haunting melody to *Taute*, the women and young girls stood in a line behind him and began singing and gently shuffling from side to side. As I fell into step with the throng of dancing men and boys who started circling Ravae, I felt the primal music's hypnotic rhythm become persistent and monotone. Each thud of the throbbing *tam tam* sounded like a pulsating heart that was beating new life into my spirit and soul. My head started spinning as the *kava* kicked in and felt like it was reviving a dormant part of my brain.
I opened up my mind, my soul, and all of my senses to *Taute* and to the voices of our ancestral spirits, but I heard and felt nothing. The air seemed to shiver with tension as we danced on and on for hours in a tireless dizzying trance, like one swirling animal, while sweat dripped from our bodies.

It might have been the effect of the *kava*, or from the biorhythm of my body being manipulated by the primal beat and feverish dancing, but I definitely felt spiritually enlightened as the intoxicating atmosphere started to fade and the throb of the *tam tam* finally stopped.

When Ravae looked to the heavens again and said an ancient chant, I slowly repeated his words and gave thanks to *Taute* and our ancestral spirits. Then when we drank another shell of *kava*, I poured some onto the floor of the *nakamal*, which is the same as spilling the blood of a sacrificial pig on the *tabu* earth, as an offering that invited the almighty *Taute* and the spirits of our *bubu* to enter my soul.

When the *kava* rite was over, Ravae cut a sliver from the spine of a sago palm leaf, burnt it in the fire, and then rolled it in ash. Then he pushed it into his bicep, and when he lit it with a burning stick, it glowed a bright orange colour as it seared into his muscle. After it festered and formed a scab, the wound would heal into a *bulu* scar.
Scarification plays an important role in *kastom*. Ravae explained that by enduring the pain in silence, he'd aroused *Taute's* compassion, and in return, the *kastom* god had empowered the *bulu* so that it wards off evil spirits and *Damate*. The villagers rely on their *bulus* for protection whenever they walk alone in jungle, which is when they are vulnerable to being attacked by a devil.

A boy gets his first *bulu* when he's about five to seven years old, and has a minimum of five holes burnt into the outside of his bicep. If he can withstand the pain, sometimes over thirty thorns burn into his flesh. A powerful spirit that will help to protect him from evil spirits enters each wound, so the more *bulus* he receives, the more resilient he becomes to the dangerous devils that live in the jungle. Young girls also receive the *bulu*.

When the sores start to heal they normally become so badly ulcerated they turn into a puss-filled mess.
Man bush believes fowl and pigs have the same blood as humans, so if a *bulu* becomes infected, an animal is sacrificed and bled into the wounds as a primitive blood transfusion. Once the animal's blood has dried, it's *tabu* to wash it off. The *bulu* can be made more powerful when a boy becomes an adult, by tattooing lines on his face or forehead with soot and a thorn from a *mole* tree.

Physically I was approaching middle age, but spiritually I was still a boy in a man's loincloth, especially when it came to enhancing my body and mind with supernatural powers.

Burning bulu scars.

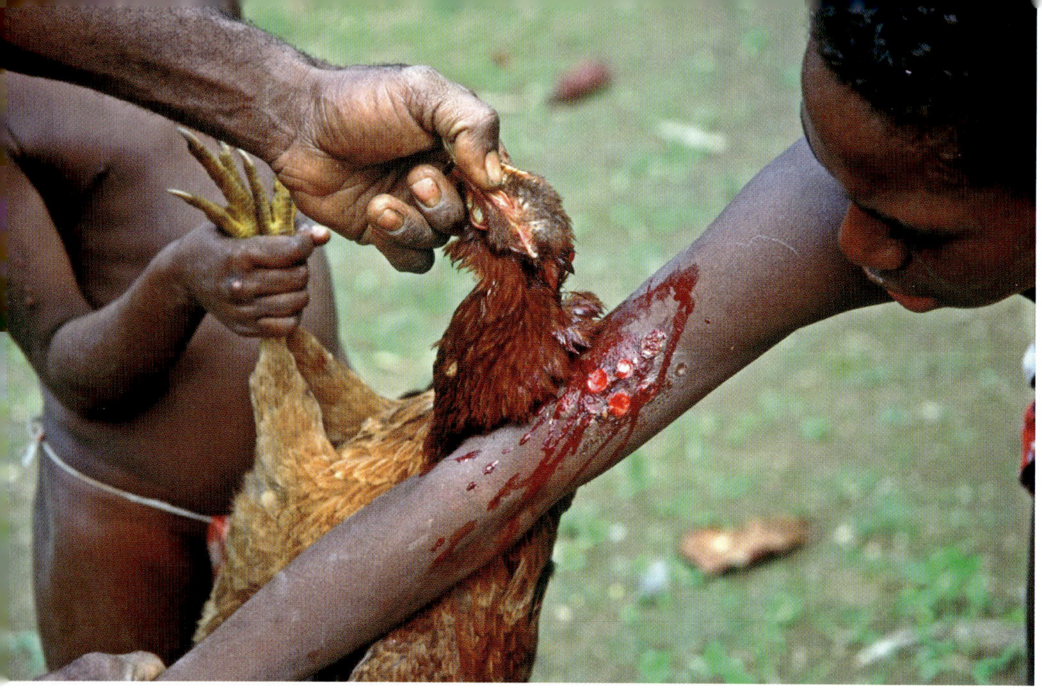

Performing a primitive blood transfusion into ulcerated bulu's.

Ravae said that as I made the transition to adulthood and became a fully-fledged man bush, when the time was right I'd get my *bulu*. After we finished celebrating with a *lafaet* and had drunk numerous shells of *kava*, my initiation was far from over. I still had to prove my manhood and my ability to provide for my clan and the community.

Killing a wild pig with a knife or a spear has never been part of a child's initiation, but then neither has smearing a thirty-five-year-old white man with black paste so the spirits think he's a man bush. When I told Ravae about other primitive cultures, he decided I had to eat wild pork, like the Dani initiates in Irian Jaya.

A few feral pigs live in a valley close to the village but they are only ever hunted when meat is needed for extremely *tabu* rituals. The reason there isn't much game in the highlands dates back millennia, to when *Taute* created Go and Sari, the first man and woman. They returned to their village after they'd been clearing a new garden all day and found a fowl and a pig that *Taute* had given them had shit inside their hut. Go and Sari were furious, and without realizing the consequences they banished them from the mountains. The disgruntled animals decided to spite the humans forever and fled to the lowlands, which is why there are only a few wild pigs and fowl living in Middle Bush.

The next morning, I was awake long before the village roosters threw back their heads and crowed to announce the start of another brilliant day. I sat outside with Garae and watched the first slithers of crimson splay across the horizon.

As the thermals were slowly energized and warmed by the rising sun, they gently lifted the mist carpeting the chain of valleys below us. Once the beautiful sunrise was over, Garae looked to the heavens and asked for guidance from *Taute* and the spirits. He pursed his lips around the *tavue*, a sacred conch shell, and blew a series of long drawn-out blasts. Their flat echo reverberated back through the ages and called upon the ancestors' supernatural powers. I filled my lungs with the cool mountain air and also blew the shell. Then we threw a sacred *oktre* leaf on the ground and stepped over it so that our quarry wouldn't see or smell us while we hunted through the rainforest.

We rubbed a wild *kava* leaf over our machetes and asked *Taute* to empower them before we tied them to sturdy saplings and made spears. Because I was single, I didn't need to worry about the *tabu* of not having sex the night before a hunt. If a hunter isn't carrying a full load of semen the spirits will hex him, the hunt will be unsuccessful, and the dogs will be torn apart by their quarry.

None of the seven hunting dogs would listen to my commands, so it was impossible for me to hunt alone. Most of the bad-tempered pack bared their teeth and looked like they wanted to rip me apart whenever I went near them. Garae's dog, Bobi, was incredibly vicious because of a ritual most of the villagers use.

The owner must be alone with the dog, and then he rubs a leaf over its muzzle and chants a spell that transforms it into a savage watchdog. Whenever I was about to enter Garae's village I avoided being attacked by shouting out Bobi's name. This made the black magic powerless, but only temporarily, and pacified the dog. Bobi had been castrated to prevent him from straying, but it hadn't suppressed the mongrel's aggressive nature, so I kept well away from its snarling jaws when we chewed a mouthful of *oktre* leaf and fed it to the dogs milling around our feet to enhance their ability to hunt.

The dogs started whining and yapping with anticipation when we followed a trail down to the lowlands. Nine hours later, after we'd travelled through prime hunting territory and had seen plenty of sign, it was obvious from the dog's disappointing performance that they hadn't hunted pigs for a long time. At the end of a long and fruitless day, we built a makeshift shelter and spent a cold night sleeping alongside a blazing fire.

We were up at dawn and started hunting after we had a nutritious breakfast of *orata* nuts and fish from a nearby river. It didn't take long for the sweat to start pouring off our bodies as we ran through the humid jungle and followed the sound of the dogs trail barking. They chased plenty of pigs, but because of their lack of fitness and the demanding terrain they couldn't catch them. When we followed a well-used pig run and our finder got a whiff of fresh scent, it looked promising when he took off with his nose to the ground and the other dogs scurried after him. As we climbed to the top of a ridge and they opened up with a chorus of frenzied barking, Garae encouraged them by screaming, "Sook, sook, sook, sook," at the top of his voice.

Whenever I've been with a highlander who's stalking with a bow it's been like watching poetry in motion. Man bush becomes so at one with the rainforest, his instinctive movements are silent and effortless, but hunting with dogs is a total contrast.

A hunter shouts, "Sook, sook," or "Cous, cous," so that the dogs become empowered with supernatural strength. Garae led the way and yelled plenty of encouragement as we recklessly bulldozed through a tight weave of jungle. While we sprinted towards the deafening brawl it sounded like all hell was breaking loose, especially when I heard an angry scoff and a piercing yelp. Then another high-pitched shriek urged us forward when it sounded like a dog had been badly wounded. Just as we were about to reach the pig it crashed off through the undergrowth with the dogs right behind it.

We raced through the tangle of rainforest and found a flattened ring of vegetation where a good-sized boar had massacred two of the dogs. One of them had a badly shattered foreleg that dangled from a thin strip of skin. I could tell from the amount of blood pumping from a deep gash in its throat that it wasn't going to survive, so I drove my spear into its heart and ended its suffering. The intestines of the other dog trailed along the ground from a huge rip in its belly. It collapsed on its side, gasped its last breath, and then died with a silent shudder. We ran towards the sound of the remaining dogs, but this time Garae wisely called them in when the boar broke from the bail. Apart from a few nicks, superficial pokes, and one badly ripped muzzle, they were relatively unscathed.

Living off the land always includes some type of violence. Something must always die so that man bush can survive, and when it does, absolutely nothing is wasted. Back at camp, we sliced off the best cuts of meat from the dead dogs, then we packed their succulent flesh inside green bamboo and roasted it to perfection in the coals of our cooking fire.

I was determined nothing was going to stop me from proving my credibility and worth, even if it meant stalking and killing a pig by myself. After we'd rested for a while we decided to hunt in virgin territory. It took our finder an hour to put his sensitive nose to good use. When the tan mongrel dropped into a wide gut and ran along a pig run, two younger dogs followed him. Several minutes passed without a sound, then two dogs that were well past their prime left our side and raced after a chorus of hysterical barking as it faded into the distance. We rushed to the bottom of the gully in a semi-controlled slide, and then sped towards the faint yapping through reasonably flat, open jungle. During our reckless chase, sweat stung my eyes and my racing heart thumped against my ribs as we struggled to keep the dogs within earshot.

While we stopped and listened at the top of a small knoll it was almost impossible to hear the dogs above the sound of our own heavy breathing. A muffled bark revived our burning legs and jaded bodies, and this time, when we arrived at the bail, the divine guidance of our ancestral spirits had provided us with much better luck. A good-sized sow stood her ground amongst the tall aerial roots of a gigantic banyan tree. She defiantly chomped and scoffed at the bailing dogs as they cautiously danced and flitted around the wide base of the tree. It was impossible to get a clear shot through the mass of roots, so I waited until the pig broke from the cover, hurled my spear, and hit her just behind the shoulder.

We sprinted behind the exhausted dogs and found the sow lying on her side about one hundred metres away. She frantically kicked and clawed the air with her hooves and then gave a final shudder and died.

Rick with the sow he killed to complete his initiation ritual.

Garae was ecstatic. He started hooting and shouting and went berserk as he tore out shrubs and kicked the base of trees while he performed the *bobo* rite to give thanks to *Taute*.
After we gutted the sow he scooped up handfuls of blood and smeared it all over the dogs. They look forward to a well-earned rest after they've been hunting and always reach the village first. When the villagers see the blood they light their cooking fires and get ready for a welcome meal of fresh meat. If the dogs swim across a river or rain washes the blood off, the villagers sniff their fur or check for the smell of blood inside their mouths.

If a boar is killed, its testicles are removed, slit open, and *tabu* leaves are pushed inside the cuts. Then one of the bollocks is held in front of the hunter's best dog and slowly moved from left to right and up and down. If the dog becomes mesmerised and follows every movement the testicle is gently thrown in the air. The hunter hopes the dog will catch and eat it. If it does, the boar's *rapee* enhances the dog's senses, and during the next hunt it can smell a pig from miles away.
We empowered our machetes with *rapee* by rubbing the pig's blood over them, and then I gave thanks to the sow and to *Taute* with a frenzied *bobo* ceremony. Garae tucked *tabu* leaves behind his ears and into his *mul mul,* and ended the rite in a more sedate way by dancing and singing to the ancestral spirits.

When I suddenly felt exhausted, I didn't know if it was from the strenuous hunt or if it was because of the gruelling leap I'd just made across a huge cultural divide.

Culture Shock

An initiation rite in Middle Bush acknowledges that a child has the spiritual awareness, courage, maturity, and skills to be an adult and a competent member of society. My initiation had been like a huge growth spurt that bypassed puberty and thrust me straight into manhood. I still had a long way to go before I became a true man bush, and had a lot to learn, but I was getting closer to the answers I was looking for.

Physically I was ready for whatever I had to face, but nothing could prepare me for the severe mental shock I was about to suffer when I became an intimate part of rituals that involve human sacrifice. Those experiences could have poisoned my soul, but I chose to make them enrich my thinking in a positive way. It demanded a lot of personal growth and at times it wasn't easy.

Now that I was an adult Ravae wanted me to have my own garden and to get married. It takes a lot of time-consuming and backbreaking work to clear one of the nearly vertical slopes where the villagers grow their food. That didn't bother me, but I shied away from the gruesome rituals that are associated with having a wife.

Gardens are made with the slash and burn method. Large trees are felled with an axe, the scrub is cut down and burnt, and then the rest of the vegetation is removed.

A wide variety of food is grown. Taro, yam, pumpkin, cucumber, *tarovit* (Fijian taro), *kumala* (kumara), manioc, *shut shut* (a leaf vegetable), beans, sugarcane, and bananas are the main crops.

A new garden is always planted while wild cane is in flower so that *Taute* will provide a good harvest, but before the crops are sown a chief visits the *tabu* cave filled with ancestral skulls. He sings to the spirits, chants into a cutting he's taken from an *oktre* tree, and then he returns and plants the cutting in the garden.

If a crop starts to look unhealthy and the leaves on the *oktre* tree are wilting, the garden is being

attacked with black magic. The *oktre* tree is cut down and at that exact moment the person that hexed the garden dies. A garden is normally weeded three times before the first harvest, and depending on what was sown, what the weather conditions were like, and a plot's size, it will usually supply food for anywhere from three months to one year. A surplus is always grown to feed friends and visitors, to help those with a poor yield, and to ward off famine during a natural disaster.

The vegetables that aren't needed are left to rot in the ground so their nutrients leach back into the soil. A plot is used for three to five years, and while it's still productive another one is always being prepared. When a garden is abandoned it reverts back to jungle for at least five years before it's cleared and replanted again.
It's *tabu* for menstruating women to enter a garden or to cook for others. Their "*rabis blud*" (rubbish blood) is believed to retard growth and to taint any food they come into contact with.

The one thing Ravae did want was a woman to come into contact with me, and in an intimate way. He felt that at thirty-five years of age I should have at least one son to continue my bloodline and look after me in my old age. Because the highlanders live as a huge extended family, if I did get married and have a child, while I was back in New Zealand the infant would be loved, nurtured, and guided by many fathers, mothers, and siblings. It would learn by example, participate in most adult activities, and develop a mature attitude and become self-reliant at a young age. I would give it a machete when it was just three years old, so it could help clear and plant its own small garden.

When I started a family my wife would have to endure the trauma of giving birth by herself. An expectant mother goes inside a hut, where she will remain in isolation for at least five days. She delivers the child quietly and without complaint, so as not to shame her clan. Then she cuts the umbilical chord with a bamboo knife and carefully stores the placenta

and its fluids in a corner of the hut. The blood and mucous covering her and the infant are *tabu*, so must stay on their bodies.
After five days have passed, if they are healthy they can leave the hut, but the afterbirth stays inside for another five days. If either of them gets sick, the mother can use medicinal leaves to relieve the pain and to drive the evil spirits from their bodies, but they must stay in the hut for another five days. When they return to their village, the rotten afterbirth is divided into equal portions, and the father, mother, and men and women from the immediate family eat it raw. The mother also drinks the vile fluids from the placenta.

Children receive their first machete when they are three years old.

I'm not a fussy eater, but cannibalising putrid human body parts doesn't send my tastebuds into a frenzy. Those who have eaten the nauseating meal told me it made their head spin, and drinking the fluids from the afterbirth made them drunk, like the *disale's* whisky. The human appetiser is followed by a *lafaet,* and either a fowl, a pig, or a bullock is killed. Then the clan celebrate their new addition to the family by ending the feast with a *kava* ceremony.

If my wife had twins, one of the children is a gift from *Taute*, and the other belongs to *Damate*. A *kastom* man holds a divination rite to decide which twin is the devil's spawn, so that it can be left in the corner of the hut and slowly die from starvation. A handicapped child requires constant care and is an unwanted burden on a clan's spiritual and physical wellbeing, so it also dies from hunger in the corner of a hut. It's extremely rare for a child to be born out of wedlock. A fatherless child is hated. None of the extended family will help to look after a bastard, so the child is buried alive at birth and always outside the hut.

Some of the other tribes I've lived with in Vanuatu told me an albino is the devil's offspring. They believe an albino's pink eyes, which are sensitive to glare, can't look up at the heavens because they are shying away from the *kastom* god. In Middle Bush, an albino is killed immediately after it's born, by whatever means the mother chooses to use. Most women shatter the child's skull with a *nul nul*.

The birth of a son is always welcomed. He will remain rooted to his ancestral land and support his parents during their old age, but a female will probably leave and marry into another clan. If a family has enough daughters, and another female is born, she's killed instantly. This controls the rate at which the population grows and helps to keep the ratio of males and females even.

Ravae understood that I wouldn't always be around to provide for a child or to take part in important family rituals, like eating rotten afterbirth. I felt a massive surge of relief when he said I should remain a bachelor. I'm a real romantic, and could never enter a loveless relationship. I never met highlanders who got married because they had fallen in love. A wife is chosen because she has the potential to produce children, will be obedient, and will work hard.

I wondered how a mother could ignore her maternal instincts, and how a selfless people that love their children could be so brutal and willingly kill a newborn baby. One night, while I sat around a fire drinking *kava* with Gramma, he told me a *kastom* story that explains how this mindset evolved, and why it's so important in Middle Bush culture.

Long ago, before the ancestors existed, *Taute* created the first men and women. The *kastom* god made two couples. Kasus and his wife were devious and evil, and Go and his partner were trustworthy and compassionate. Kasus wasn't satisfied with just one woman and lusted after Go's wife. While Kasus and Go were hunting for pigeons they saw a hawk flying back to feed its young. They watched it disappear into a deep crevice that dropped down into the bowels of the earth. Kasus tied Go to a *kastom* rope and lowered him into the hole to capture the young hawks. As soon as Go was out of sight, Kasus cut the rope and knew that Go couldn't survive the horrendous fall.

Kasus returned to the village and told Go's wife her husband had slipped into the crevice and died. Then Kasus married Go's wife, but Go had somehow managed to survive his terrible injuries. He ate the young hawks, but after being trapped in the chasm for weeks he was dying from starvation. While he was delirious *Damate* entered his dreams and told him if ants bit his flesh he must shut his eyes and endure the pain without uttering a sound.
If Go saw a hawk soaring overhead, he was to stand completely still and close his eyes. When an army of vicious ants and the bird entered his dream he ignored the intense pain when the ants attacked him. When he woke up he was overjoyed.
An *orisina* tree had grown up to the sky. He climbed out of the crevice, returned to the village, and hid in the garden, where he stayed until he'd eaten the last of the bananas. While the others were inside their hut he crept up and quietly opened the door. Kasus told

his first wife to go and see if they had a visitor, and when she went outside Go cut off her head with a *jaike* (stone axe). Several minutes passed, then Kasus ordered his second wife to see what was taking the other woman so long. Go decapitated her as well, then he did the same to Kasus when he stepped outside. When Go murdered his wife and members of his own bloodline he'd fed their sacrificial blood to the devil. *Damate* was pleased with Go and made him the first *matia*, so that for the rest of eternity society would accept that a good man could also be evil.

Throughout Vanuatu the *kastom* men who use sorcery to kill or to manipulate other's lives are known as *nakaimas*. In Middle Bush they are called *matia*. There are different types of *nakaimas* on Santo. Some dig up the bodies of babies that are starting to decompose, break open their chests, and then eat their fetid hearts. Others exhume human bones and use them to manipulate the spirits and to cast evil spells, but this doesn't make them a true *nakaimas* because it only gives them limited powers. The most feared and potent *nakaimas* are the *matia*.

Matia and *nakaimas* learn their dark and extremely secretive craft deep in the jungle. An initiate must endure a lengthy and brutal apprenticeship called "the *tabu* fire." They preform horrific rituals in hidden caves, amongst the massive roots of remote banyan trees, and in other *tabu* places. They indulge in inhuman acts around a *tabu* fire, eat raw rotten meat seething with maggots, and wallow in fetid juices dripping from the bodies of villagers that other *matia* have killed. The *tabu* fire got its name for a number of reasons, but mainly because an initiate lives off food roasted in a sacred fire. They also eat animal excrement and their own putrid shit and they survive on dirty water. This is an absolute necessity, as it conditions their mind and bodies for what lies ahead of them.
An initiate must fully understand the cycle of nature. The *tabu* leaves and the other types of vegetation that they use for black magic are alive with divine power. They all have unique characteristics that can create different links to the supernatural. A *matia* must learn when the best time of the year is to use the leaves, when they will be most potent, and how the ebb and flow of nature can affect their magic. They also learn how to use spirits that live in stones and other *tabu* objects.

Matia are taught that the body is comprised of three key components, the flesh, the spirit, and the soul. Flesh is biological and is the unfeeling mechanical part of our body that keeps us alive and functioning. The spirit is the most vital of the three. It gives us desire, leads us, is our conscience, and determines our actions. The spirit is the very nucleus of mankind's being because it survives after the body dies and travels to the next dimension in the other world or it stays in this world.

Ravu Magic. One of the highland's most potent cannibalistic *matia*.

The soul is a living entity that feels physical contact and then communicates with the spirit. The spirit has total control over the soul, so for example, if you touched your arm, the soul feels the contact and relays the message to your spirit so that you know your arm has been touched.

There are two kinds of *matia*. The first *matia* spirit was created in another country and lived inside a *tabu* box while it travelled through the spirit world to get to Santo. Thousands of years ago, a highlander befriended the *matia* spirit and became its first owner. Then he performed a ritual that uses the juice of a green coconut so that he could pass the *matia* spirit on to men and women.

An initiate can also receive a *matia* spirit from a *matia* while they are alone in a *nakamal*. The *matia* makes a huge *tabu* fire, then throws the initiate into the flames. If a *matia* spirit pulls the initiate out of the fire and he hasn't been badly burnt he becomes a *matia*. If he can survive the brutal rite five times he lives a long life and will be protected from some of the rituals the villagers use to kill a *matia*.

The most common and more potent type of *matia*, *Tauko Lomo Lomo*, originated on Santo. When an initiate is ready to take the final step to becoming a *Tauko Lomo Lomo* he travels through the jungle until he sees an animal. Then he returns to his hut and falls asleep so his subconscious can enter the other reality. If a naked old man with white hair and a long white beard enters the dream he teaches the initiate everything else he needs to know to become a *matia*. When the ancient spirit shows him how to kill, he learns how to bang two coconuts together, how to use *tabu* leaves, how to sing deadly *kastom* songs, how to use a black woven basket filled with *tabu* leaves while he holds it in his hand or wears it around his neck, how to use a *kastom* axe or *tabu* knife, how to use powdered human bone, and how to murder his victims with numerous other rituals.

When the initiate wakes up he is empowered by the *matia* spirit, but to become a true *matia* he still has to complete another gruesome ritual. He has an inescapable craving for human flesh and an insatiable thirst for human blood that can only be satisfied by killing someone from his own family. To show *Damate* that he feels no remorse and is worthy of becoming a *matia*, he kills a relative, eats the heart, drinks the blood, and cannibalises the body.

Children are loved by everyone, but their hearts are highly prized by cannibalistic *matia*.

Now I fully appreciated why Gramma had warned me never to walk around at night by myself. The threat of being cannibalised lurks everywhere, and is a constant danger. When an initiate completes the final step he becomes the devil's eternal disciple. If he doesn't keep feeding *Damate* with human spirits and flesh and blood, then he becomes the sacrifice and the devil kills him. No one is safe from an attack.

Newborn babies and young children are especially vulnerable because their hearts have the most potent *rapee*. Once a victim has been chosen and the *matia* calls upon the powers of the spirit world, it's like lighting the evil fuse of a time bomb. He has a specific amount of time to feed his master, and knows that if he fails he will die. If his victim escapes, if need be, he will kill another *matia*. The body parts and the spirit of each victim make him more powerful, but this also puts him at risk. There are no achievable levels for a *matia*, but as he becomes more potent, his bones and organs become more desirable to other *matia*, so he also lives in a world filled with insecurity and danger.

Ravae increased his powers by using an ancient bone from the little finger of one of the most dangerous *matia* who ever lived. He made a cut in his chest, pushed the bone inside the muscle, and then cauterised the wound with a burning stick.
A *matia* always wears a beard, as this is a vital part of the ritual that enables him to become embodied in an animal's flesh. This is how most children are killed. The *matia* possesses an animal, then makes it walk across the path the child uses everyday. The child dies the instant it steps where the animal has walked. Whenever a *matia* murders an adult he uses a *tabu* knife to divide the heart, flesh, and blood into equal portions, and then he usually shares his grisly meal with other *matia*. Any woman who is about to be killed is raped first during a ritual called *masing*. A spirit turns her screams for help into a silent gasp by overpowering her voice, which is controlled by the soul.

The villagers are absolutely terrified of being killed by the sound of two coconuts being banged together by a *matia*. The victim falls to the ground unconscious, then *Tauko Lomo Lomo* asks, "How do you want me to dismember your body?" When the victim replies, "Cut me here," the *matia* knows which limbs to sever and dissects the body with the precision of a surgeon.
After he drinks the blood and eats the heart, he replaces the heart with a small green coconut. Sometimes the intestines are removed and the empty stomach cavity is filled with leaves. Then the *Tauko Lomo Lomo* leaps over the body and says to the victim's spirit, "How long do you want to live?" While the *matia* performs a complicated ritual, he sings to the spirits, milks the juice of *tabu* leaves into the body parts, and carefully puts the corpse back together. The victim returns to the village and seems normal, but for the next five days he is one of the living dead, a zombie, until he suddenly dies on the sixth day.

Traditional society couldn't function properly without the *matia*. Their main role is to maintain spiritual and social harmony by manipulating the supernatural and using powerful magic. They sometimes perform feats in front of the villagers that are so amazing they command instant respect. Witnessing this power first-hand creates fear and awe and eliminates the need for prisons or police. The villagers know that if they break a serious *tabu* their chief might ask a *matia* to call upon the dead to kill or discipline the living.

The community accepts that the ritualistic murders are a normal and essential part of *kastom,* so they treat a *matia* as a respected and loved *kastom* brother. But if a *matia* feeds the devil with more sacrifices than are needed, the villagers retaliate. Sometimes they plant arrowheads around their huts and on the trails that the *matia* use. These cause terrible wounds that leave a blood trail, so the *matia* can be tracked down and killed.

As the days turned into weeks, I was always vigilant, but one of the things I couldn't protect my body from was everyday life. Although I thrived on the hardships and loved the challenge of embracing a primitive lifestyle, it wasn't if I became sick, it was when, how badly, and would I survive, because while I lived like a man bush I committed some form of hygiene suicide every day.

The highlanders are naturally tough and energetic, and their children and elderly are generally much fitter and stronger than in a Western society. While I watched mothers chew food and feed it to their infants it transmitted germs that built up the child's immunity against diseases. Adaptation and aggression are the keys to surviving in Middle Bush, and my body was still adapting to the living conditions.

I received my primitive vaccinations by catching the tropical diseases that lingered in our hut. Even walking across the floor in bare feet and standing in the slimy patches of spit and bacteria-infested snot either made me sick or helped build up my antibodies. The huts are basic, but they aren't squalid. They were swept and cleaned regularly, and the villagers kept clean as well by washing every day.

Our diet also took a heavy toll on my health. Most nights, we shared food from a large communal pot or ate off a *lap lap* leaf. Sometimes Voemanu would pinch the snot dangling from the children's noses, flick it from her fingers, and then use the same hand to give me a piece of food. Although that's nothing compared to some of the vile things I had to eat, no one in their right mind

Food is normally shared from a communal cooking pot.

Kastom demanded that Rick commit hygiene suicide by eating rotten meat.

would willingly jeopardise their health like that, especially in such a remote location. I had no other choice. If I complained or refused to eat with my family I'd be treated like a social outcast or banished forever.

Because of the lack of game in the highlands, any type of meat is a luxury. I shuddered whenever we killed a bullock to top up the village pantry. The bulk of the meat was wrapped in *lap lap* leaves, then roasted in hot stones. It was recooked over and over, and normally smelt so vile when it started to rot that I could barely get past the smell to put it in my mouth.
Some of the meat was cooked inside bamboo, and six weeks could pass before the fat-stained bamboo was pulled from the hut's rafters and split open.

Eating rotten meat made me violently ill, but there were much worse meals. One of the worst is part of a ritual where meat is hung in the searing sun until it's seething with maggots and oozes dripping juices. The juices are caught in a bowl and the nauseating concoction of maggots and fetid fluids are mopped up as a gravy with a piece of taro. Then the rotten meat is eaten raw. Everyone has to take part in the repulsive feast, and when they do, vomiting is *tabu*. I was told the rite is simply a necessary part of *kastom*. Because cannibalism, becoming a *matia*, and several other rituals forbid vomiting, the ceremony probably prepares the villagers' already cast-iron stomachs for these sacred occasions.

The fowl that were always trying to sneak inside our hut are a precious item, so we usually only ate them during rituals. The dogs were always sneaking inside as well to scavenge for scraps of food. If they were lucky they tipped the lid off a pot and quickly lapped up its contents before someone screamed "*kesa*" ("get out") and gave the poor animal a swift kick or a thrashing with the flat side of a machete. We still ate any food that was left in the pot, and in leaner times we ate the dog as well.

Most nights our hut was full of hardcore drinkers who shared Peta's thirst for strong *kava*. Trying to keep pace with them also wore down my resilience and stamina. Sometimes we started an all-night session by drinking a shell of *blud* (blood). This potent cocktail is made by sieving a small shell of incredibly strong *kava* into a larger shell that contains normal *kava*. If I was given a rusty tin mug that was filled to the top, it had the same effect as a shell of *blud*. I nicknamed it "bulldozer," because it flattened me and all of my senses. After my third bulldozer I always had double vision and fell into a hypnotic trance. When we were drunk, and while everyone connected with the spirit world, our hallowed silence or our hum of quiet chatter was usually interrupted by the sound of gushing vomit.

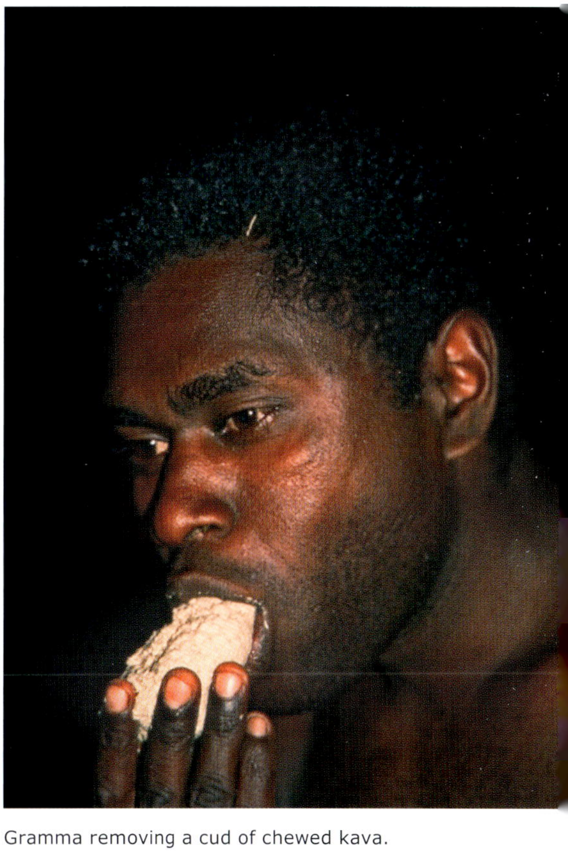

Gramma removing a cud of chewed kava.

Some of us would make it to the door in time so we could throw up on the *tabu* dance ground, while others would leave huge puddles of vile-smelling spew on the floor of the hut. During a really big night we binged until everyone threw up, then we started drinking again. Whenever we got drunk and vomited it was part of an important ritual that demanded the utmost respect. When vomit is laced with *kava*, is has *rapee* that creates a strong link to the ancestral spirits and to the supernatural.

The more *kava* I drank the more vivid my dreams were. Some of the nightmares I had were so real and so dramatic I woke up lathered in sweat and breathing heavily.

Even after a heavy session of drinking *kava* it was difficult to sleep. Sometimes the fires in our poorly ventilated hut belched out smoke that was so thick it felt like you could chew on it. This is why most of the villagers suffer from respiratory complaints. The smoke was always worst during times of sickness, when Peta created a dense fog to confuse any devils that might be trying to invade our bodies and make us unwell while we slept.

The symphony of farting, loud coughing, and the drone of snoring echoing around our hut also made it hard to sleep. When the rats came out of hiding and started scurrying across the rafters their high-pitched chatter or the piercing sound of their fighting woke everyone up. While the rodents foraged for scraps, our pots clanked and rattled until someone swore and threw anything within arm's reach at them.

Man bush never sleeps with a blanket. The only thing that keeps their virtually naked bodies warm are the fires next to their sleeping mats. The days were hot but the night air had a chill that constantly nipped at our sleeping bodies. When the cold shook me awake at least two or three times a night, I breathed life back into my fire and hugged its flames until I felt warm enough to try to go back to sleep again.

The annoying insects that crawled all over me while I was trying to doze off also made it difficult to sleep. I didn't mind the cockroaches that ran through my hair and all over my body, but the other insects that used me as a smorgasbord were a nuisance. I always resisted the urge to scratch their bites, as they loved feeding on weeping sores.

I never woke up in the morning feeling fresh and energetic, even after a good night's sleep. If we'd binged on *kava* I always felt hung over for the first few hours, and I'd start the day with a headache from sleeping in a cloud of smoke.

Most mornings we were up before the sun, had breakfast, and walked to the gardens that cling to almost vertical slopes. During the strenuous hike we asked *Taute* for strength by singing *kastom* songs, by yelling the long drawn out *kel* call, by whistling, and by being happy. Working in the garden absorbs most of the villagers' time and energy, so a carefree attitude helps to lighten the heavy workload. Whenever we shouted the *kel* call, which was often, and it echoed around the valleys, we were empowering each other with *rapee* from our ancestral spirits.

Towards the end of the day, after digging, weeding, clearing the jungle, or gathering crops, the women recharged their jaded and aching bodies by singing to *Taute*, while the men drank a shell of *kava* to get strength from the spirits.

Carrying taro back to the village.

We all carried heavy loads of vegetables back to the village. The men always take less than the women, and everyone relieves their pain during the hard climbs by rolling their tongues and cooing softly like a pigeon, to ask *Taute* to give them strength. It always amazed me when I watched young children carry a small load of crops as far as their still developing legs would take them. The three-year-olds struggled sometimes, but the four-year-olds normally made it all the way back to the village.

As each day passed and I kept getting weaker, it wasn't because of everyday life. A tropical disease that lurked in my system was gaining momentum and growing stronger. One morning, while I followed Gramma down to his garden, I knew something was drastically wrong when I struggled to keep up with him. We'd almost reached the garden when a wild dog suddenly leapt into the middle of the trail. It snarled and snapped at the air and looked like it was going to rip us to pieces. Gramma screamed and swore at it, so I followed his lead and called the crazed animal everything under the sun. When it showed no fear and stood its ground I wondered if its strange actions were caused by rabies or some other illness.

The villagers coo like a pigeon to ask the kastom god for strength when they carry heavy loads.

Gramma knew what was wrong. The spirits were making his body shake uncontrollably, to warn him that the dog was possessed by a *matia*. Our flurry of foul language had asked *Taute* for his protection, because anyone who's bitten by a devil dog suffers a terrible death and has their body mutilated. We could try to kill it with our machetes or run.

Gramma screamed, "Run, Tavua!" then he spun around and sprinted back up the trail as fast as his legs would carry him. I managed to stay right behind him until we hit the steepest parts of the trail, where even walking was a marathon effort that made our legs burn. When I staggered through the door of our hut I collapsed in a quivering heap, and while I gasped for breath, to avoid having to submit to a painful exorcism ritual, I reassured Gramma I hadn't stopped along the way. His fear of the devil and a massive surge of adrenaline had energised him so much that he'd sprinted most of the way back to Nukurekum.

While I was still struggling up the steep slopes, he'd already performed a ritual in the *nakamal* to protect us and the village. He sang into a smouldering fire, and then he frantically kicked pieces of glowing wood aside and scooped up handfuls of warm ash, which he scattered around the hut, around the village, and on the track leading up to the village.

Then he sprayed mouthfuls of water in the same places, and for added protection, while I lay on my back with my hands over my pounding forehead, he spat water over me, in case *Damate* had invaded my body while I'd lagged behind.

That night, when I quietly succumbed to a hellish bout of malaria, it wasn't the devil that had made me ill. I was glad that everyone slept while the fever violently shook my body from head to toe. *Damate* always preys on the weak first. After our close encounter with the possessed dog, I knew the villagers would put me through a painful exorcism ritual if I showed any signs of sickness. That was the last thing I needed. I was way too sick to ignore my instincts when I decided contacting the pygmies would have to wait, so after I medicated myself I told Gramma it was time for me to head back to civilization.

If Gramma hadn't carried my largest pack down to the lowlands I definitely would've collapsed on the side of the trail. The Jordan River was in flood so we had to take a long and tiring detour through the undulating jungle. By the end of the day I felt so violently ill and so exhausted, when we stayed in a small village I slept alone in an empty hut.

This deeply offended Gramma and our hosts, but it felt like something was trying to smash its way out of my head with a ten-pound sledgehammer, and I didn't want to shame my clan by complaining or Gramma to think I was possessed by *Damate*. When I curled up on the floor I muffled my moans with my hand and waited for sleep to put an end to my misery.

The next morning, Gramma was furious. I'd committed a huge breach of *kastom* by sleeping in another hut. My punishment was simple but incredibly harsh. I couldn't hide my sickness any longer, and although it was obvious I needed help to get to a hospital urgently, Gramma took me to the edge of the Jordan River, said goodbye, and then walked away.

I followed the river to the start of the nearest road, then my frail legs buckled and I slumped to the ground and passed out.

The rest of my journey seemed surreal. A massive bullock with a reputation for being aggressive tried to attack me, and when I finally reached the Lappe River, a flash flood had swept away a hut where I knew I could get help. When I staggered to another village my delirious body was placed on a bamboo slat bed, then the villagers nursed me while they waited a few days for a pickup truck to take me to Luganville. It took four days in intensive care at the hospital, then another week of bed rest at John Noel's, before I was well enough to go and live with a tribe on another island.

Gramma driving devils from the village. The arc of colour in the spray is believed to be a spirit.

Death and Destruction

Almost a year later, when I returned to Nukurekum a nameless fever was ravaging Middle Bush. A cyclone had cut a destructive path through the mountains, destroyed most of the crops, and left an inevitable outbreak of disease in its wake. When I entered our hut everyone looked and sounded sick, and Peta was so unwell he literally had to drag his emaciated body from his sleeping mat when he tried to offer a warm welcome.

It was hardly the perfect start to another stint in Middle Bush, especially when Peta started shaking violently from a bout of malaria. Voemanu locked the doors to the hut and then stoked the fires until the air was filled with a blinding fog of thick smoke, so the evil spirit she was about to exorcise would be confused when it left her husband's body.

Peta was so delirious, and his chills were so bad, he tried to warm his quivering hands by putting them in the fire. Voemanu screamed and wrenched him away from the flames, then she gently eased him onto his back, straddled his trembling body, and spat on his stomach. After she viciously massaged the spit into his torso, he gasped and tried not to moan when she drove her thumbs into his belly button. Her battle with the devil that was trying to kill her husband was nearly over. She scooped a handful of smouldering ash from the fire, sang into it, and used it to anoint Peta's body. Then she looked to the heavens, sang a chant to *Taute*, and asked his powerful spirit to drive the devil from Peta's soul. When the ritual was over, Peta curled up into a quivering ball on his sleeping mat, and I went outside and filled my lungs with cool fresh air. No one ever enters or leaves a hut during a healing ceremony. They are terrified that if they do, the demons that are being exorcised will kill them and everyone else in the hut.

During my absence the inevitable winds of development and change had also swept through the highlands. Some of the villagers who welcomed me back were wearing filthy ragged clothes so they could keep warm at night. Ravae looked absolutely ridiculous dressed in a frilly woman's blouse that was inside out and two sizes too small for him. The biggest change had started in Luganville, while Gramma was there completing a course with the Red Cross. When Garae visited him, a minister from the Protestant Mission had lured Garae to Christianity.

I was stunned that someone with such a firm belief in *kastom* had embraced the religion of a culture that he absolutely hated. He convinced his chief that education and the medicines the Protestants had promised him would enhance everyone's lives, so the villagers built a new leaf hut at Vanakanakarea that could be used as a church and school.

Only a handful of converts were attending the services every Sunday, but the Protestant Mission wanted a Ni-Vanuatu minister to come and live with the highlanders. I knew that if those plans went ahead, a culture that I thought I could only ever dream about finding would be destroyed forever.

Peta performing a healing ritual on Tutino.

Over the next few days, several *kastom* men went from hut to hut and performed healing rituals. They told their patients it was *tabu* to eat pablemous, coconut, sugarcane, and bush cabbage, and it was *tabu* to wash until they fully recovered.

The sour stench of rancid body odour filled our hut and got so bad I could almost taste it. When some of the villagers became seriously ill, several cures were used to try to heal them. Peta crawled from his sickbed and held leaves over a fire until they were smoking hot, then he rubbed them over the body of a four-year-old girl. As soon as the leaves seared her skin she screamed and writhed from the pain.

I watched a woman make a poisonous broth by mixing wild *kava* roots with boiling water. Then she sang into the potion, asked *Taute* to expel the demons from her body, and drank the scalding hot mixture in one hit. When a mother treated her young son with bark from the *pasa* tree, she boiled it, poured the broth into her mouth, squeezed her son's cheeks together to open his mouth, pressed her lips on his, and then blew the piping hot mixture down his throat. While he clutched at his burning neck she massaged his stomach and slammed her thumbs into his navel. These were brutal cures, but one of the most damaging was the *tabu* of not being allowed any fluids after a healing ritual. Some of the villagers were critically ill, but they didn't drink water for days.

One of the sick infants in our area really suffered. His pain was treated with pain during the *kova* rite. A child normally endures the harrowing ritual the first time they get sick after their third birthday. A *kastom* man performed the operation in the afternoon, with a bamboo knife, which cut away pinches of skin in two vertical rows on the child's torso. While five men held him tight to stop him from squirming, the *kastom* man scraped the yellow fat from the wounds with the end of the knife.

Because the child was seriously ill, it received twenty incisions to make sure the evil spirits were bled out properly. After a sacrificial fowl was bled into the wounds to replace the lost blood, the cuts were covered with a poultice of medicinal leaves. The child's stomach was so tender he walked hunched over for a week, as standing upright was too painful.

When I caught the fever and collapsed, Peta looked so sick I wondered if he was going to survive. He normally put his potent *rapee* to good use and performed our healing rituals, but he barely had enough strength left to move, so I asked Ravae's brother, Ravu Magic (Ravu), to heal me. Ravu is the most feared and respected *matia* in the highlands.

The way he easily lived up to his reputation as being the wildest man in Middle Bush absolutely fascinated me. He had a powerful middle-aged body, devilish beard, and a hypnotic stare that felt as if it could pick you up and slam you against the wall. From the first time we met, I was instantly drawn to his charismatic personality, and by asking him to cure me, I sealed our already firm friendship.

Two weeks later I was exhausted and emaciated, but I was grateful to have survived the lethal sickness. While I sat outside our hut and recuperated in the warm sunshine, I heard Gramma's wife crying from an excruciating headache that starts off the illness.

She obviously thought that apart from Peta, we were alone, and just as Gramma returned from working in the garden she let out a long groan. He didn't approve of his wife's moment of weakness, and gave her a loud slap in the face and then hurled abuse at her for shaming her bloodline with her noisy suffering.

The vicious fever was hard on the young and the elderly. If a child died in another village, the news always raced along the jungle telegraph at a blistering pace so that we knew to keep away. The next morning, the father expresses his grief by arming himself with a bow. Then for one full day, using highly exaggerated movements, he stalks the village in search of victims. No one is safe. Even unsuspecting visitors are fair game. Everyone stays inside their huts, as deaths occur during this grim ritual.

During my previous visit, Gramma had asked me to help him set up a basic clinic, which is why he'd completed the Red Cross course in Luganville. While I was back in New Zealand I started a charity called The Vanuatu Child Aid Foundation and managed to get a two thousand dollar grant to supply him with medicines. His basic knowledge of administering medication may well have saved the life of an old woman who died in a nearby village, but like most of the highlanders, she chose *kastom* medicine over the *disale's* magic pills and paid the ultimate price. When I keeled over from another dose of fever I was way too sick to even think about attending her funeral.

Her body was laid on a woven mat inside her hut and surrounded by mourning relatives, who held *nagria* leaves while they continually wailed and cried for three full days. Then she was decapitated, her was skull was placed in the *tabu* cave, and the rest of her remains were buried inside the hut. During the next ten days, her family held a feast, where everyone ate at the same time and skewered the food with sticks, as it must never touch their hands. When the feast is finished the deceased's spirit flies up to the sky and into the realm of the supernatural, to a beautiful heaven where no one gets married. Hell doesn't exist. Everyone goes from the physical world to a nirvana filled with boundless love and eternal harmony, where no one wants for anything. When a villager's spirit has crossed over to the other reality, a sacred bird sings outside their hut. A spirit can only return once of its own free will in the form of a white ghost. After that, those who know how can summons it, but it can't be seen, as it has no size, shape, or form.

Everyone's body receives the same send-off except for a chief. His immediate family has the choice of two rituals to use and decides which is the most suitable. First the corpse is smoked over a fire to remove the body fluids, and then it's laid flat on the firewood rack inside his hut, directly above the cooking fire, where it remains for one hundred days. Then the head is severed and stored with the hordes of other skulls in the *tabu* cave.

In Western society, at a wake we drink a toast to the dead. In Middle Bush, the send-off is much more personal. They literally drink the dead. The rest of his remains are cremated, then the ashes are mixed with water and drunk by his relatives, so they become empowered with the chief's potent *rapee*.

The other funeral rite for a chief has such a strong *tabu* that if anyone with different beliefs views the body he is killed on sight. The cadaver is smoked on a platform inside his hut for one hundred days. During the first five days, the relatives sit beneath the corpse and wail and cry while they hold *nagria* leaves. Then for the following ninety-five days, only the men sit beneath the body, which they do each night when they eat, and drink *kava*. Throughout the one hundred days a piece of dry wild cane or an arrow is placed in one of the cadaver's hands and set alight. The flame is never allowed to burn out and is constantly transferred to another piece of cane or to another arrow. At the end of the one hundred days, the head is severed and placed with the other ancestral skulls. Then the mummified body is buried alongside the central post inside the hut. Both of these funeral rites end with a huge feast.

Peta's health had deteriorated so much that I wondered if he was going to survive. If he died, because he's the second most powerful *kastom* man in Middle Bush, there was a strong possibility Gramma would join him in the spirit world. Gramma told me he would try to inherit his father's potent *rapee* before the corpse was used for the funeral rite.
The body is laid on its back in a hole approximately two and a half metres deep. Then from the first dusk after the death until the following dawn, he would lay face up on top of Peta's corpse. If it wrapped its arms around Gramma's chest he would receive all of his father's *rapee*. But if Peta's spirit pushed Gramma off of the body during the night, then he would leave the hole on daybreak without becoming empowered. If Gramma did receive Peta's powers he would live a long life and he couldn't be killed by violence or by a *matia*. But first, he'd look death in the eye when either his uncle, who is the first choice, or any another male villager, armed himself with a bow and stood ten to fifteen metres away. Then Gramma would use a *nul nul* to try and ward off a barbed arrow aimed at his heart and fired from full draw.

When a young girl from another village died from the fever, her father was adamant that someone had killed her with black magic. The chief of the girl's bloodline drank a shell of *tabu kava,* then he visited the ancestral skulls, and after a highly secretive rite, the spirits revealed the murderer's identity. When the chief told the mourning family who the killer was, *kastom* demanded that they seek revenge, but this unusual ritual also compels them to be compassionate. They told the murderer the spirits had sentenced him to death, and allowed him to flee into the jungle. Then they vented their anger by attacking his hut with axes, to give him and his family time to escape before they burnt down the hut. His family sought refuge in another village, but he wasn't safe anywhere. He was banished from his village and hunted relentlessly for one full cycle of the moon. The grieving family tried to shoot him full of arrow holes and tried to club him to death with a *nul nul*, but he managed to survive. When he returned to the village everyone forgave him, helped build his family another hut, and welcomed him back as a loved *kastom* brother.

While I slowly recovered by relying on traditional healing, Peta also relied on *kastom*, and stubbornly refused to take any *disale* medicine. As each day passed his face became gaunt, his eyes sunk into their hollow sockets, and his body wasted away. *Taute* and the spirits weren't being kind to us, but no one dwelled on our plight or found fault with the gods.

Kastom had demanded that throughout my sickness I survive solely on tarovit and water. It didn't take long for the inadequate diet to take a heavy toll on my health. When I recovered, I welcomed the addition of bush cabbage, which had been *tabu* during my illness. There were other crops that survived the hurricane, but I never complained about my poor nutrition, in case there was an underlying reason.

Even the weather was being unkind. Several weeks of unrelenting rain had transformed the normally clear rivers into thundering stretches of dirty brown water that were impossible to fish. Although these were lean and testing times, no one was going to die of starvation, as the cyclone hadn't destroyed our plentiful supply of *tarovit* and taro. It would've been easy to flee back to the comforts of civilization, but apart from a more healthy diet, I wanted for nothing. Instead of becoming preoccupied with food, I focused on life's simplest pleasures. I savoured the warmth of a fire, loved being enveloped in contagious laughter, enjoyed a mellow *kava*-induced high, and wallowed in the highland's beauty and serenity.

The resilience and uncomplaining outlook of man bush washed over me. I took a leaf from their book, and instead of being fresh-faced and unenlightened in my own comfortable society, I chose to look and feel like hell, so that I could experience the lows as well as the highs of life in Middle Bush.

One of the highlights of my day was eating a cat's back leg. Gramma skinned the feline by making a small incision in its pelt with a slither of bamboo. Then he pushed a hollow piece of bamboo into the cut, and blew through the tube until the skin pumped up like a balloon and separated from the carcass. Unless you've been violently ill and have had to survive on a basic diet, its probably hard to imagine the effect that hunger can have on your mind and body. I developed a craving for rat. The Middle Bush vermin are healthy-looking animals, unlike the disease-ridden grey rodents that live in the towns. After I shot one with a bow or caught one in a trap, I cooked it like the villagers do. I singed the fur, scraped it off with a bamboo knife, gutted it, peeled the skin off the tail, and roasted it over a fire. Whenever a rat scurried across the rafters my mouth started to water. It's also the children's favourite food. They love the taste, and it's part of an important ritual that instils them with the nimble rodent's *rapee*, which makes them agile and gives their legs strength when they travel through the rugged mountains.

I had a good rapport with all of the children. The highlanders' strong sense of unity and their devotion to their families has a flow-on effect. Because the children receive so much love they become extremely affectionate towards each other. I never saw them fight or have venomous arguments. They groomed my hair for lice as a sign of friendship and affection and revelled in being allowed to touch a *disale* while they spent ages curiously running their fingers over my body.

One afternoon, I decided to surprise a small group of kids that were hanging around me. When I said I was about to perform *disale* magic everyone stared up at me with wide inquisitive eyes and hung on my every move.

First, I told a small boy to pull my finger, and when I farted everyone went into hysterics. After the giggling eventually stopped, I called for silence and turned my back on them. I pulled my two top false teeth out so they stood out like buck teeth, tucked my hair behind my ears, and blew out my cheeks. Then I pulled my ears out wide, widened my eyes, and spun around and faced everyone while I made a deep moaning sound.

Some of the panicked children tripped over one another as they screamed and ran for their lives from the white devil. When I burst out laughing, once the others got over their initial shock, they literally rolled around on the ground with laughter.

For the rest of the day I was visited by adults and children that kept asking me to make my "monkey face." When poor Vetrivu saw my contorted features, she shrieked, shook from head to toe, and was convinced I was *Damate* because I'd pulled my teeth out and then put them back in.

Some of the children were too sick to come and see Tavua's magic teeth. When Gramma's three-year-old son, Tutino, collapsed with a fever, Peta crawled from his sickbed and performed a healing ritual.

For the next two days, when Tutino became delirious and slipped in and out of consciousness, I feared the worst, but the resilient child slowly recovered after Gramma combined numerous healing rituals with modern medicine.

The epidemic ended, and the devils that caused our sickness were purged from the village, but my hardships had only just begun.

Gramma's son, Tutino.

Sometimes the bow is used during life-threatening rituals.

The Exorcism

The bow and arrow has played an important role in shaping Santo's fascinating history. To man bush it's much more than just a weapon, it's a spiritual object filled with great power. I'd brought a modern hunting bow with me so that I could help to keep the village pantry full.
The first time I shot it for the hordes of curious villagers, nearly everyone reacted in the same shocked manner. Whenever an aluminium arrow hissed through the air and sunk into a black palm target, their eyes bulged and their tongues poked out, then they looked at one another and began whooping and jumping with joy. It was as if they were seeing someone let rip with a scud missile for the first time.

When the news about my bow travelled from village to village, curiosity eventually got the better of one of the pygmies. He trekked across the mountains to visit me, but he'd also come to celebrate Tutino's recovery. We were so happy the evil spirit had been cleansed from Tutino's frail body that we sang and danced and drank huge amounts of *kava*. As we whirled around the fire to the seductive beat of throbbing *tam tams*, now I had two reasons to party.

Even if we didn't share an interest in archery, the moment I saw Atison I knew we'd be good friends. He looked like an African pygmy, loved to dance like they do, and his smiling eyes, cheerful personality, and raucous laughter stood him head and shoulders above the throng of sweating dancers.
Atison looked at me and yelled, "Tavua, tomorrow we go hunting," then he stomped the ground and twirled around in a dizzying circle. After I nodded an enthusiastic yes, I stumbled over to a wall and rested while my mind buzzed from the invitation and from drinking way too much *kava*. When another shell of the brain-rattling brew was thrust into my hands, as soon as I knocked it back everything became surreal. I bounced off the walls of the hut, staggered over to a sleeping mat, and collapsed in a drunken heap. Then I curled up into the foetal position and despite the noisy singing and the ebb and flow of the persistent *tam tam*, I instantly fell asleep.

The next morning, I regretted waking up with a raging hangover as I picked my way through a maze of bodies strewn across the floor and stepped outside to perform the *bobo* ceremony with Atison. After we climbed down the greasy slopes towards the lowlands, when the terrain slowly levelled out, the continuous rain had transformed the track into a leech-infested, ankle-grabbing bog.
We left the trail and entered an undulating expanse of reasonably open jungle with a good population of pigeons and flying foxes (fruit bats).

I relished the opportunity to see how Atison hunted with his primitive bow. Thousands of years of evolution have made his tiny body perfect for travelling through the rainforest. As he quietly led the way, I fell into silent step behind him and became spellbound when I watched him transform from his usual carefree self into a serious hunter. For the next half an hour, we stalked through the lush forest until we heard the gentle cooing of a nearby pigeon. Atison stopped and then expertly mimicked the bird's call while he softly chopped his throat with the edge of his hand. The pigeon responded with a noisy whoosh of feathers as it flapped to the top of a nearby tree. I couldn't see it, but Atison didn't have any problems picking out its iridescent plumage from amongst the weave of leaves and branches. When his arrow struck a tangle of growth shielding most of his target, the pigeon erupted with a flurry of feathers and flew across the valley.

During the next couple of hours, while we silently moved through the jungle, two more arrows rattled through the branches and narrowly missed plump pigeons that were gorging on berries or drinking nectar from flowering trees.

While we walked to a nearby river, Atison pointed to a flying fox soaring through low clouds and quietly said in an excited voice, "Tavua, garae, garae!" ("Tavua, flying fox, flying fox!") As we reached the riverbank, an *isio* bird (kingfisher) shrieked its distinct call. Because we were standing face to face, it meant the bird's cries came from over Atison's left shoulder and over my right. It was a good luck sign for my little pygmy friend, but a bad omen for me.

For the next uneventful hour we stalked downstream by crossing back and forth through the river's foaming waters. When we quietly walked around a bend in the riverbank Atison suddenly stopped mid-stride and slowly crouched down. His keen eyes had instantly seen a flying fox that was fast asleep and hanging from a branch in a *bulacho* tree about fifty metres away. He crept forward with deadly silent footfalls that were as fluid as the waters tumbling over a small waterfall below us. A huge smile spread across my face as I watched him glide to a stop seven metres from the dozing flying fox. His muscles danced beneath his ebony skin when the limbs of his bow stretched to full draw, and when the arrow flew through the air one of the three arrowheads humanely sliced through the bat's head.

My little friend was ecstatic. His eyes shined and were filled with bliss as he started whooping and wildly flailing his arms. He shouted, "Oh, Tavua! Now we will eat well my brother," then he ran towards the tree where he'd shot the bat, kicked its trunk with the sole of his foot to express his joy, and roared with laughter. While he gave thanks to the bat and rubbed its blood into a small notch in his bow, to reap its *rapee*, he was still grinning from ear to ear.

For the next fifteen minutes, he danced and smirked and gazed up to the heavens as he sang and thanked *Taute*. I fell into step alongside him and broke out into a wild dance to express my gratitude to the spirits and to share in Atison's happiness. His joy became so infectious, and I laughed so hard and for so long, I ended up rolling around on the ground in hysterics. We were deep in the jungle, in our own little world, and more than happy to be in it.

After we'd gathered succulent *meme* stalks and bush cabbage to eat with our flying fox, we decided to go and roast our kill at a *tabu* waterfall called Poroua. While we were pushing through knee-high grass a slight movement caught the corner of my eye. A large brown Pacific boa was slithering alongside us so I grabbed a sturdy stick and whacked it across the head.

As soon as Atison saw me holding the snake his lips quivered, then the rest of his tiny body started shaking. He had every reason to be frightened. *Damate* sometimes inhabits the body of a snake, and although I didn't realize it at the time, I'd just committed a serious breach of *kastom* by killing the reptile at the base of the sacred waterfall.

Atison was absolutely terrified of snakes but he still agreed to drape it across his shoulders and pose for a photo on a rock face alongside the waterfall. Just as I cranked off the last shot, the ground shuddered and then I heard a loud rumbling noise that sounded like distant thunder. Because we'd had weeks of incessant rain, I thought we were about to get hammered by a flash flood, so I screamed out "Run!" to Atison but I needn't have bothered. He'd already scrambled across the waterfall and over a fern-covered bank before the words of warning had even started spilling from my mouth.

By the time I grabbed my camera and tripod it was too late. Massive chunks of rock exploded from the face of the waterfall and rained all around me. When the noise suddenly fell silent, it reminded me of the abrupt and eerie calm after a loud and unexpected car crash. We looked at each other nervously, burst out laughing, and joked about how lucky we were to be alive.

Atison with the snake Rick killed.

I'd lost an alarming amount of weight while I was sick. My body desperately needed protein, so when Atison singed the fur off the flying fox I threw the snake into the fire. Anyone else wouldn't have hesitated to tell me I'd broken another tribal law when I ate the snake, but Atison treated me with an almost subservient respect.

Sometimes primitive peoples can be incredibly difficult to understand, but it still doesn't explain why he never warned me that snakes living in a *tabu* place are never eaten. Any that are caught in the jungle are fair game, but because of the villagers' fear of *Damate*, and because it's common for them to get sick after they eat snake, most of the highlanders' won't touch them.

A geologist would probably have a rational explanation as to why the rock face exploded. Atison believed that supernatural powers rather than the forces of nature were responsible. The spirits were angry and had tried to kill me with the hail of rocks. During the walk back to Nukurekum Atison became grim-faced and never said a word.

My honest mistake created havoc when the news raced from village to village. The nervous shouts, the anxiety, and the looks of terror on some of the faces made me think about Busa's threat to cut off my genitals if I broke a *tabu*. Everyone gave me a wide berth. They were adamant *Damate* had become embodied in my spirit and soul. I was no longer a human, I was a devil. Peta was still gravely ill and barely able to move. He didn't have the strength to deal with my dilemma so he sent a runner to get Ravu.

Ravu sped to our hut and started preparing for an exorcism. I knew a ritual this important required me to wear a loincloth, so I tied one on and readied myself mentally. When I saw Ravu chewing a huge mouthful of yellow, "two-day" *kava*, I raided the nearest cooking pot and gorged as much bush cabbage and taro as my stomach could hold to help reduce the brutal effect of the *kava*. Ravu led me to my sleeping mat, then I gulped down mouthful after mouthful of the vile-tasting brew until I finished the massive shell in one hit. The fires had been stoked so much that a stifling cloud of smoke choked the air and made it hard to breathe. When Ravu started singing to Taute and held a sturdy-looking branch of wild *kava* in his hand, I braced myself for the intense pain I was about to suffer.

The *kava* kicked in just as Ravu lifted his arm above his head so that he could whip my back as hard as he could. The branch bit into the flesh on my back and then I was flayed from head to toe to drive out the devil. Then my vision doubled, my body started shaking violently, and I collapsed in a quivering heap and wanted to vomit. I fought the nausea and held onto the ground when the floor began to rock, and while the hut reeled, my brain started spinning around inside my skull. It felt like I was floating in a turbulent ocean when Ravu sat on my hips and spat huge globules of phlegm in my face and on my stomach. When he viciously drove his thumbs deep into my navel and a wave of pain swept through my body I refused to wince or show any sign of weakness. The sound of his monotone chanting was the last thing my traumatized senses registered when I mercifully drifted into unconsciousness.

I spent the next two days (which is how the *kava* derived its name) in a paralytic coma. I pissed myself, shit myself, and had the most hellish nightmares imaginable. I was so far gone, and so helpless, I couldn't even brush off the insects feeding on my unwashed hands and lips. As soon as I awoke I blew a cockroach from my nostril, then I nervously reached down and felt for my penis and my testicles. I smiled when my manhood was still intact, and sighed with relief when I saw the evil spirits hadn't been bled from my stomach. My body still shook all over and I was a mess, but I was grateful Busa hadn't inflicted the cruel sentence he'd promised. Voemanu was horrified when I snorted the cockroach from my nose, and was convinced she'd just seen a devil leave my body. She sent for Ravu, so that he could perform another less painful ritual to purify my tarnished soul.

Gramma was furious. As he walked towards me he raised his voice and warned that I'd shamed everyone from my bloodline. Then he said I was lucky that Busa had been told my breach of *kastom* had already been dealt with. Once he cooled off, he sat on a log beside my mat and said, "Tavua it's hard to know everything about *kastom*. I'll tell you more about your bloodline." Although I belong to the flying fox clan and I have a powerful spiritual bond with the nocturnal mammals, I'm still allowed to eat bat. In the past, the eight villages worshiped the taro, pig, flying fox, spider, fire, water, wild taro, and the owl. Nowadays, because of intermarriage and the alliances the villages have formed, some of the clans share the same totem.

The flying fox bloodline originated when a bat flew into an unmarried woman's hut. She was alone, so the bat fornicated with her, and she gave birth to a son who became the first male of the flying fox clan. The highlanders call one of the species of black palm *wuluwulu garae*. One day a man heard a small girl crying while he walked through the jungle. He climbed to the top of a ridge, where *wuluwulu garae* always grows, and found a small girl who had been abandoned by the devil, nestled in the fronds of a black palm. He held her in his arms, and because the palm has the same name as a bat, he shouted, "*wono garae*," ("you are of the flying fox"). Then the children married each other and formed the true flying fox bloodline.

Whenever a highlander passes through a village that shares the same *kastom*, taking food from a vacant hut is welcomed and expected. Because I'm from the flying fox clan, I always left a small branch from the *arabous* tree above the front door, so the occupants knew their food hadn't been stolen and from which bloodline the hungry visitor belonged to.

Our totems are also linked to the cockroaches that were crawling over my body during the exorcism ritual, which explains Voemanu's horror when I blew one from my nostril. Most of the huts have small numbers of the insects, but members of another totem have cursed the villages with heavy infestations. Gramma said nowadays Winea is free of cockroaches but in the past it was alive with them. Busa's mother, Notsan, inherited the curse from her own mother, and when Notsan died, the cockroaches mysteriously vanished.

Up until 1994, Ravae's hut had crawled with them, when the curse had been passed onto Vatious, Ravae's grandmother. The plague was so bad that cockroaches rained down from the rafters and made it difficult to eat and drink. Everyone spent more time picking them from their food than they did eating, so in the end, Vatious ate the vile insects as well. When she died, the cockroaches suddenly and inexplicably disappeared from her hut.

Vatious passed them onto her relative, Voemaburu. She's our neighbour, and lives with her son, her sister, and her brother-in-law. They were always civil to us, but by highland standards they were the neighbours from hell. Voemaburu and her sister are a rarity in Middle Bush society, where screaming, swearing, and disputing over petty items is frowned upon. They constantly argued, and things got so heated one day, Voemaburu chased her sister and tried to hack her to pieces with a machete. If they weren't quarrelling, a continuous tangle of chatter drifted across to our hut. Peta called them *tongan* (noisy), and was always telling them to keep quiet.

Everyone in our hut went into hysterics when I jokingly shouted they had mouths big enough for two sets of teeth and to shut up. Until Voemaburu had been damned with the cockroach curse, Nukurekum was almost free of the annoying pests.

Winea

It had taken the highlanders three years to give me enough knowledge and experience so that when the time was right I'd be ready to visit Winea. When Atison sent a message across the mountains to Nukurekum, my little pygmy friend had finally oiled the hinges to the closed door that I'd patiently been waiting to open. Garae's words were sheer bliss when he smiled and said, "Tavua, Ravu will take you to Winea tomorrow." I was still a mess from the brutal exorcism, so when he mentioned I'd be going pig hunting with two of the pygmies, I thought about the state of my health. The wild shaking in my hands had healed to a slight tremor, and I felt sluggish and had chronic diarrhoea, but it wasn't going to stop me from visiting the pygmy village to continue my search for the answers I hoped to find.

Late that evening, when Ravu sat next to my fire and unwrapped a bandage of leaves from his finger I could smell rotting flesh. He wiped the blade of my pig-hunting knife on his *mul mul* and then he pushed its razor-sharp edge through the wound and carefully sliced away the decaying tissue. Then when he dipped a piece of coconut husk into some boiling hot coconut oil and dribbled it onto the open wound, his head swung from side to side, he screwed his eyes shut, and he gritted his teeth while he fought the pain in total silence. He endured the brutal remedy several times, until the steaming fluid completely covered the wound.

Ravu would've used a bamboo knife to cut away the evil spirit that was responsible for his puss-filled mess, but he was so impressed with my knife he decided its keen edge would be more effective. Voemanu finished off his treatment with a healing ritual, then she tied *tabu* vines around his wrist and biceps to stop the sickness from spreading throughout the rest of his body. He guzzled down a shell of extra strong medicinal *kava*, and within minutes he was fast asleep.

The next morning, after we blew the *tavue* shell to tell the spirits we were heading to Winea, the tiresome slog through the waterlogged terrain was hard on our unhealthy bodies. When we reached the Lappe River, the rainforest had lived up to its name, and weeks of heavy rain had transformed the normally gentle flowing current into a boiling surge.
We traipsed downstream to find a quieter stretch of water, but even then we made a hazardous crossing.

When Ravu craned his neck and looked up at a steep climb, he said, *"Tavua, kevoro. Yumi mas go first time."* ("Tavua let's go. We must go quickly"). *Kastom* required us to run up the sheer ridge as fast as was humanly possible, without resting, until we reached the halfway point, where in the past a sentry was always posted. While I tried to keep up with his blistering pace it pushed my endurance to its absolute limit. When we finally rested against a tree at the halfway point, Ravu casually wiped the sweat from his eyes, smirked at my deep breathing, then rolled a cigarette and commented on how strong I was.

From this lofty vantage point it was easy to see how a sentry could cast a watchful eye across the valleys and basins and search for approaching enemies. When he blew a *tavue* shell it gave Winea's inhabitants plenty of time to prepare for an attack. Winea translates to "to eat man," and was given its grisly name because the pygmies enjoy eating human flesh. They have such a violent reputation that I wasn't surprised when Busa had told me a white man hadn't visited the village for nearly a century. He'd also said that when he was a young boy tribal warfare was rampant and danger lurked everywhere. The *matia* and their enemies posed such a huge threat that everyone returned from their gardens before dusk and locked themselves inside their huts. The tiny pygmies commanded so much respect, and were so volatile, all of the villages throughout the rugged interior were terrified of them. Even nowadays anyone who enters their territory unannounced invites certain death from a hail of arrows.

In the past, the villages in the surrounding valleys were tired of living in constant fear, so they united, and under the veil of darkness, a swarm of heavily armed warriors made the difficult climb to the remote hamlet. One of them crept ahead and expertly dispatched Winea's inattentive sentry with a well-placed arrow.

During other paybacks, only enough blood was spilled to please the spirits, but this time none of the pygmies were going to be spared. During a horrific massacre, a few of the pygmies saw the futility of trying to fight back while they were so grossly outnumbered, and fled into the jungle and survived. The captives were put in a bamboo cage on a grassy knoll above the village and were roasted alive. Then the triumphant enemies celebrated with a cannibal feast.

Ravu Magic blowing the tavue shell before heading to Winea.

Smoke from the cooking fires rises through the thatch roofs of Winea's leaf huts.

The handful of men and women who escaped from the brutal attack managed to rebuild Winea. Then in a cruel twist of fate, they succumbed to a tuberculosis epidemic that swept across the highlands. Busa and his people survived the disease by chewing medicinal leaves and using healing rituals.

While I enjoyed the captivating views and the raw beauty, I thought it was ironic that Busa, one of the archipelago's smallest people, ruled the highlands from the island's highest inhabited peak. The surrounding mountains and valleys are covered in dense rainforest, but Winea's knoll is bare and carpeted with short grass. As we entered the village, I felt exhausted just thinking about how the pygmies make the exhausting climb up and down the sheer face every day to reach their gardens.

When Busa walked out of his hut and pointed his bow at me, I took serious heed of his harsh warning to wear a *mul mul* next time, and knew he wasn't joking when he said that no matter how hungry I was, he would kill and cannibalise me if I ever ate a snake at a *tabu* site again. Then he put his bow aside, smiled, and asked if the snake tasted good. Once his chiefly duties were over, he greeted me as a long lost brother would.

This was a very different paramount chief from the one I'd met before. He was more open and much friendlier, but beneath the welcoming smile, there was an aloofness that demanded I treat him with respect. Atison stepped outside and was followed by two other pygmy men in their early thirties. When Silas and Matai introduced themselves, they were emotional and cheerful and weren't afraid of my skin tone. As they both welcomed me with a tight hug, Matai made clicking noises with his tongue and looked up at me with an affectionate smile.

I could see my bow was making them wild with excitement, so before we entered Busa's hut for a welcome ceremony, I gave them a quick archery exhibition. When I fired several arrows I couldn't help but laugh at their astonishment, but it was nothing compared to watching them shoot the bow. It was an unforgettable and hilarious experience.
We all roared with laughter when the diminutive archers broke out into an expressive and joyous jig whenever they fired an arrow. When they poked their tongues out and their eyes bulged it was way too much for me. I literally fell over laughing and tears of joy rolled down my cheeks.

Although my pint-sized friends were all heart and couldn't have offered a warmer greeting, their fierce reputation is justified. While Matai and Silas chewed our *kava*, Busa told me about Winea's fascinating history. During the 1950s and up until the 1960s, it was unthinkable to travel through the highlands unarmed. Most villagers slept with their weapons handy, or even tied them to their hands. The threat of an ambush lurked behind every tree, and attacks from enemy clans were commonplace. Several decades later, the skirmishes became less frequent, but even now fighting still occurs, and traditional enemies are viewed with suspicion and contempt.
Busa's father, Calico Mia, hunted the victims for the most famous cannibal feast in recent times. After a solo one-hour trek to Nambamba village, he shot and killed three men with his bow. To have faced the enemy village alone is a tribute to his incredible bravery and is why his exploits will always remain legendary. Then in an amazing display of stamina, he carried the bodies back to Winea by himself, and prepared them for a feast.

This ritual has strict *tabus* that are never broken. The bodies were tied to poles and stood upright in front of Calico Mia's hut. Then when he placed his hand on their hearts to reap part of their *rapee*, no one else could touch the bodies for one full day. After they were cooked whole in hot stones, he obtained their full *rapee* by eating their hearts and smashing a hole in their skulls and eating their brains. While the bodies were staked out in the sun the flesh had started to decay and smell. *Kastom* demands a clan must eat everything that their hardened systems can digest, until the whole carcass is finished.

Busa remembers the feast vividly, and in a matter-of-fact tone said that by the time only three skeletons remained, the vile meat reeked, had turned dark, and tasted so repulsive he almost vomited. If anyone had failed to keep the gruesome meal down, they would've suffered a horrific death from the victim's regurgitated spirit. This *tabu* also helped to prevent indiscriminate murders, as killing the enemy is supposed to be measured and have a definite purpose, so that an entire clan is never slaughtered. Unlike most of the other islands throughout Vanuatu, where only the men ate the dead, the women willingly joined in the grisly meal. Vetrivu fondly remembers eating the flesh of Calico Mia's victims.

Busa is proud that he's a cannibal, simply because it's such an integral part of *kastom*. By carrying on his father's legacy as a fearless warrior, his courage and ability to fight has become legendary throughout Middle Bush.
Although I tower over him and weigh ninety kilos, his size ten feet are wider than mine, his hands are the same size, and his powerful calves, thighs, and biceps roughly mirror my athletic measurements. His power-to-weight ratio is incredible.
To have the stamina to single-handedly carry a fully-grown man who was dying from malaria, all the way to an aid post in the lowlands is an amazing feat. And to have the skill to fight off two much larger men who launched a surprise attack and clubbed him to the ground three times with their *nul nuls* is equally remarkable. He had a severe wound on his forehead, but he still managed to find his feet a fourth time and knocked both men out cold with his bare fists.
Gramma said when he'd travelled with him through the lowlands a stick had stabbed right through Busa's calf muscle. Without even a grimace, Busa casually pulled the stick out, treated the injury with herbal *kastom* medicines, and covered the gaping wound with a bandage of *lap lap* leaves. Then he carried on walking as if nothing had happened and made the torturous hike all the way up to Winea without complaining.

Busa explained that he's only aggressive when it's a part of *kastom*. He exudes a natural inner calm and is a remarkably intelligent and fair man, who willingly listens to others before he makes his own decisions. His most important role is to maintain spiritual harmony throughout the highlands, but if anyone foolishly crosses him or disrespects *kastom* he'll kill them in a heartbeat. A helicopter pilot and his passengers discovered that when they landed on the grassy knoll above Winea. While Busa told me what happened, I thought about the sheer arrogance and stupidity of landing a helicopter in the backyard of a primitive people that hasn't had any contact with outsiders. The chaotic noise and the downdraught terrified the women so much that they shook and started to cry. They were too afraid to look outside and cringed in the corner of their huts while Busa and the other men raced towards the chopper with their bows. If the women had seen the devil fall from the sky with the *Damates* sitting inside it's belly, they would've been completely overwhelmed. The men weren't afraid. They were going to kill and eat the intruders if the helicopter pilot hadn't jumped back in his machine and flown off. There are only two pygmy women left, and the insensitive intrusion had a lasting impact on them. They've never seen a white man, and the news that a *disale* was coming to Winea terrified them so much, they fled to a hut down in their gardens.

Ravu had watched a helicopter "fall down" beside the Lappe River. While he raced through the jungle towards the hovering chopper, he was convinced its pilot and passenger were about to steal gold from the river. He threw a rock at the canopy and narrowly missed the pilot, who wisely took off at high speed. Ravu wished he'd had his bow, or better still, a musket to kill the thieves. Some of the other villagers had seen a helicopter land on several occasions and for some reason thought they were Australians trying to steal gold. If the highlanders ever catch them, they've already planned how they will kill and eat the thieves.

When Busa said, "That's enough stories, Tavua. We will drink *kava* and sleep," I wished he'd kept talking for hours. Although we were in an incredibly remote location, and night had fallen, Atison barricaded the doors. If anyone enters or leaves a hut while Busa is drinking *kava* they believe the spirits will make another villager kill them in a violent manner. Ravu and I were still feeling unwell, so after a few shells of *kava* we drifted off to sleep as soon as we stretched out on our sleeping mats.

At three in the morning, when I rushed into the nearby jungle with diarrhoea and vomiting, the last thing I'd expected was to suddenly feel a supernatural presence. Sometimes I thought I felt something during extremely *tabu* rituals and whenever I was in a *kava*-induced trance, but here, the spirits were tangible. When I told Busa what I'd experienced, he merely nodded his head with an expression that said I was beginning to understand what it is to be a true man bush.

Ravu Magic with Rick's ancient three-piece bow.

Winea is the spiritual heart of the island. If a highlander is murdered anywhere on Santo, his spirit travels to the knoll above the village and screams a warning.
In the past, this gave the pygmies time to prepare for a possible attack. Anyone who has travelled beyond Winea, deeper into the interior, has said the jungle is alive with spirits. They hear noises coming from a village of the dead. Babies cry, men shout, and even the sound of the *tavue* shell reverberates through the rainforest.

The next morning, when the *tavue* signalled the start of our hunt it stirred me from a deep sleep. Ravu was shivering and lathered in sweat while he lay on his mat.
It looked like he was suffering from one of the jungle's numerous fevers or because the infection had spread from his finger. He wasn't going anywhere in his sorry state, so I stepped outside and joined Matai and Silas in a *bobo* ceremony.

When I followed them into the predawn darkness and walked through a steady drizzle of rain, the tiny archers were so confident that the spirits would give us good luck during our hunt they only carried three arrows each.

Back at Nukurekum, whenever I'd travelled through the jungle, I'd been praised for my agility, but as we headed towards the lowlands, I felt like a cumbersome giant while I struggled to keep up with the nimble pygmies.
They casually leapt from one foothold to another down almost vertical muddy slopes, and wherever we could, we jogged through the difficult terrain.

Four hours later, when we only had a brief rest to eat *nakavika* berries and edible fungus, I knew I was being tested, or that Busa was making me pay for eating the snake.

By mid afternoon we'd reached our hunting ground. We travelled through the jungle at a swift pace, and at the end of a luckless day, when dusk fell we lit a huge fire to keep *Damate* and the other devils away. The dismal weather soaked us to the skin as we stretched out on a bed of *lap lap* leaves and tree fronds. Throughout the night, we woke up shivering and took turns stoking the fire and hugging its flames until the rising sun warmed our bodies.

Running in wet pants had chaffed my crotch, and overnight the tender rash had turned into a weeping mess that made walking painful. By late in the afternoon we'd covered a lot of country without coming across any game. When the persistent rain finally stopped and we found the fresh footprints of a small boar, Silas tracked it with the skills of a bloodhound. He trailed the prints along a gentle sloping ridge that twisted down into a messy gully filled with fern. As the sun ended its daily voyage into the horizon, a cloud of mist descended and left a damp sheen on our skin.

When the light started to fade, Silas moved with a sense of urgency when he bent down and parted the fern to look for sign, until a muffled grunt and a rustle about thirty metres away brought us to a sudden halt. Silas quickly nocked an arrow and switched into predator mode. His lithe body seemed to almost flow along the pig run while I held back with Matai and watched. He stopped mid-stride several times, with his foot poised above the ground, and held the motionless pose whenever the fern became still, then he carried on when it started shaking and the pig began rooting and feeding again. He expertly narrowed the gap to about eight metres, then slowly rose from a crouch, shuffled slightly to get better positioned, and pulled his bow to full draw.

As the deadly arrow flew through the air, Silas was almost right behind it. The startled boar scoffed and threw its head back when the arrowhead sliced into several vital organs. As it spun around and fled on a surge of adrenalin, Silas flew through the air and landed on top of the pig. He knew that trying to track an animal in darkness in country this rough would've been impossible.

The next day, we jogged to the base of the climb up to Winea, ran to the halfway point, and kept running until we reached the village and divvied out the pork. Ravu was back on his feet after shaking off his fever, and I'd gained Busa's respect by going on the exhausting hunt while I was clearly unwell.

While we rested our weary bodies the following day, I was surprised to learn that most of Nukurekum's and Vanakanakarea's inhabitants originated from Winea. When a cyclone flattened the village centuries ago, most of the pygmies decided to move from the exposed knoll and built new huts on the ridge tops of the surrounding valleys. Over the years, intermarriage has ensured they are destined to become extinct. Busa's wife comes from another village and is almost six feet tall. As a consequence his son towers over him.

I would never have thought Ravae, Peta, Vetrivu, Voemanu, Ravu, Gramma, and numerous others were born at Winea. None of them look like pygmies, but their bloodlines have evolved from the pygmy gene pool.

When we returned to Nukurekum, that night, we heard that a highlander had been beaten to a bloody pulp while he was in Luganville. Whenever the villagers travel to town to sell *kava* and buy a few basic items there is always an element of danger. Most of them do their business and return to Middle Bush as soon as possible, because of the ongoing feud with the people from Mantantas. The hatred between this coastal tribe and man bush started when the "sol wota" (salt water) people became jealous of the vast amounts of land the highlanders' own. Nearly everyone I spoke to had been in a bloody brawl while they visited town.

The pygmies are expert hunters.

Ravu had chased a mob of men from Matantas down the main street after they threatened to kill him. He brandished his machete, and was disappointed that they managed to outrun him when he tried to hack them to death. Gramma had broken his hand and arm when he fought off two men who ambushed him. He warned me to be wary if I was in Luganville with any highlanders.

Peta was still riddled with malaria, and the *tabu* of not washing had made his body odour so rancid that even a maggot would've gagged. Some of the tribes in Vanuatu believe eating goat meat cures malaria. When Gramma asked me to join him on a wild goat hunt, even though my groin was weeping puss, I would've shamed my bloodline if I refused to help my *kastom* father.

I knew I was still being tested when he said, *"Yumi go longwea small,"* ("We will go a fairly long way"), and I knew it was going to hurt, especially in country this rugged, and especially when *kastom* required us to capture the nimble goats with our bare hands.

We were away early the next day. We jogged all the way down to the Jordan River and hunted in terrain that was so jagged and dangerous, I had to concentrate on every step I made. As we crept towards a mob of feeding goats a vigilant nanny stamped her foot and snorted a loud warning. When they took off and we sprinted after them, my heart pounded so hard I could feel it beating a tune on my eardrums. As we sidled across a sheer face I slowed down to a fast walk, but Gramma was as agile as the goats we were chasing and kept running after them. He caught up with the tiring animals as they ran uphill, and managed to wrestle a medium-sized billy to the ground. About twenty minutes later, after I followed the sound of his *olau* call, I found him hanging on to the goat under the shadow of a giant wild taro plant.

After Gramma gave thanks during a frenzied *bobo* ritual, *Kastom* required us to carry the goat back alive, without tying it's limbs together, as this cuts off the circulation and destroys the meat's *rapee*. The irate goat bleated and thrashed about on our shoulders when we took turns carrying it during the gruelling walk back to the village.

When we reached Nukurekum, Gramma slipped a noose around the goat's neck and hung the struggling animal from a sturdy tree limb. After it gave a final shudder, he slit its throat, gave thanks to Taute, and smeared blood all over his body to gain its *rapee*. Any meat from below the goat's knee is *tabu* and can be eaten only by the hunter, so that it empowers his legs for the next hunt. I felt exhausted but elated after the long and tiring day. Gramma had gained immense respect as a hunter, I'd passed another test, and Peta had plenty of nutritious meat.

Peta made a slow but steady recovery, and when he was well enough, he acknowledged the hardships I'd quietly endured by asking me to perform an *essengo* rite with him and Ravu. The simple rituals were a huge honour that gave me an inseparable alliance with two of the highland's most respected and powerful men.

Over the next few days I felt it was definitely time to leave. Peta became irritable and seemed to be suffering from some type of post-fever depression. When I followed him and Voemanu to the garden to take a few photos, it nearly ended in disaster. As soon as I raised my camera he screamed abuse and threatened to cut me up with his machete. Gramma was standing nearby and whispered, "You go, Tavua! Now before he kills you!"
I took heed, and before things got really ugly I put plenty of distance between us.

Some of the tribes in Vanuatu believe eating goat meat cures malaria.

I'd been lucky, because a year earlier, Peta could kill simply by yelling. Numerous villagers told me they'd witnessed the phenomenon, when pigs, fowl, a bullock, and even a nighthawk that was flying overhead were killed by his shouts.

Peta was worried he might lose his temper and kill a villager, or even worse, a family member, so he performed an exorcism rite to get rid of the deadly spirit he used. I could foresee serious, if not fatal problems arising. If I got on the wrong side of Peta I knew he wouldn't hesitate to kill me, so I decided to leave the next morning.

Matai and Gramma came with me to Luganville to sell their *kava*. While Matai went to buy something by himself, four men from Matantas tried to attack him.

He knew he was no match for his burly opponents and used his brains instead of his tiny brawn. He ran for his life, and when we eventually regrouped and went looking for the men, *kastom* demanded that we beat them until their bones broke and their blood flowed. We looked for several hours then gave up when we couldn't find them.

My search for a new pair of inner soles for my boots was so hilarious I doubled over with laughter. The only place that sold them was a chemist, and when I told the woman behind the counter I needed a size twelve, she acknowledged my request with a nod and handed me a large tube of haemorrhoid cream.

My crutch was still healing, and I'd waddled into the shop, so she mistakenly thought I said arsehole instead of inner sole. From the way I painfully walked with my legs bowed, it felt as if that part of me needed replacing, but it still puzzles me how she knew what a size twelve looked like and how much cream it would take to heal it.

I spent a couple of days resting at John Noel's, then I visited a tribe on Malakula Island. When I collapsed from a hellish bout of malaria, I became so violently ill it took months to get well again. If I'd known that the next time I returned to Middle Bush the after-effects I was still suffering from were going to put my life at risk, I would've waited until I made a full recovery.

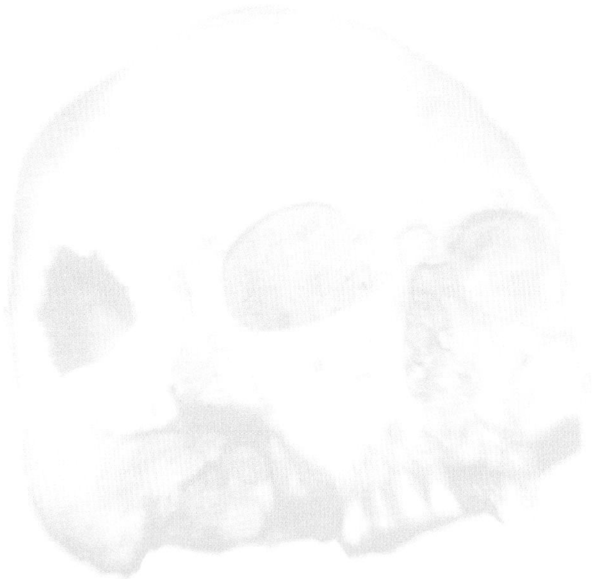

Busa is proud of his cannibalistic tendencies.

The Winds Of Change

The bout of malaria I survived made me dyslexic and damaged my memory. Whenever I tried to remember anything about the highlanders I constantly had to refer to my notes. It took three months of slow recovery before I could write an article that made any sense.
When I returned to Vanuatu the winds of change had swept through Middle Bush when *kava* prices skyrocketed to an incredible twelve hundred vatu per kilo. John Noel became a *kava* agent and earned an easy one hundred thousand vatu (Vanuatu's currency) per tonne. He was buying two tonnes a week, and making huge money compared to the average weekly wage of three and a half thousand vatu. A gold rush mentality surged through the islands when instant fortunes were being made.

I met Ravu in Luganville, and while we waited for a ride inland he told me that before the price of *kava* escalated, some of the people in the urban areas had looked down on man bush. They thought of them as being impoverished, unhygienic, and savage heathens. The highlanders' huge *kava* plantations were a goldmine. They knew some of the civilized Ni-Vanuatu had always mocked or despised them behind their backs. A few boisterous natives walked down Luganville's main street and laughed at the expatriate businessmen, the industrious Chinese traders, and the Ni-Vanuatu who worked as labourers on copra plantations or did other menial tasks.
Young boys who had never had any real concept of the value of money became instant millionaires by selling their entire *kava* crop. The hotels and bars in Luganville overflowed with primitive men wearing loincloths who squandered more money on alcohol than they would have made in an entire lifetime. There were plenty of shrewd opportunists who capitalized on the *kava* boom by borrowing huge amounts of money from hopelessly drunk natives, when they never had any intentions of repaying them.

Some of the natives were traumatised when they realized they'd made huge amounts of money. An old man from South Santo who had been destitute all of his life started shaking when a bank teller pushed a pile of notes towards him. He cried and screamed and then left his money sitting on the counter and ran away. It took a while for his son to calm him down before they returned to gather his riches.
Another elderly villager from Pentecost Island fainted and collapsed on the floor of the bank when he was given a massive wad of notes. The boom lasted for a year, and then when the government foolishly sold *kava* plants to America, Hawaii, and Mexico, they established a niche for themselves in what had previously been an uncompetitive market. The government should've retained ownership of the world's most potent plants and marketed the cultural significance of the *kava* as well.

A teenager about to plant kava cuttings in his garden.

While some primitive peoples quickly frittered away their instant wealth, Busa had a good business head. When the highlanders accumulated millions of vatu, he called all the chiefs together and they unanimously agreed to invest their combined profits as a down payment on a new Toyota pickup, to be used as a taxi. They also chose a driver and he moved to Luganville so that he could get his license.
I was amazed, because there were members of some clans who had never seen a white man before my arrival, and now they owned shares in a pickup. During one of my previous visits I'd followed an old woman that walked down from the mountains for the first time. When she saw a truck she thought it was a monster that had swallowed the villagers sitting inside. She curled up into a quivering ball and rocked backwards and forwards until someone explained that she had nothing to fear.

It took a while to get my head around one of the world's most primitive peoples being the proud owners of a brand new Toyota. When Ravu and I left Luganville on the back of a new white pickup with "Winea" painted on its side, he told me other changes had occurred in Middle Bush. A teacher and his wife from The Protestant Mission Service had been living at

Vanakanakarea. They'd convinced more of the villagers to wear ragged Western clothing and the children wore clothes whenever they went to school. The Christians had stopped working in their gardens on Sundays so they could go to church and to show respect to Jesus and God. About thirty worshipers attended each service, and some of them travelled vast distances through the jungle to get there. The teacher's wife became so terrified of the highlanders she fled back to Luganville. Then when the teacher visited his wife and borrowed the school's only calculator, to man bush this was blatant theft, so they made it known if he returned he'd be killed on sight.

Then the Protestants sent Stephan Vavanaru and his wife to Vanakanakarea. Stephan found the first few months incredibly difficult. The constant fear of being killed and the stress of worrying about his wife frayed his nerves. His wife was so petrified she fled back to her own village, but Stephan put his faith in God and stayed behind to try to end the barbaric rituals and to try to convert and educate the highlanders.

While I was away, another church had tried to impose its beliefs on the highlanders. As we bounced along the badly potholed road, Ravu used a mixture of Bislama and broken English and said, "Tavua, two *disales* stop on top close up die finish." If Stephan hadn't tried to convince the villagers that killing another human being was wrong and ungodly, two American missionaries in their mid-twenties definitely would have died.

A grossly overweight woman and a reed-thin man had followed a Ni-Vanuatu guide to Nukurekum. By the time the exhausted woman staggered into the village, she needed to be supported under her arms to stop her collapsing. A gale force wind that blew driving rain into her face washed away the tears that were streaming down her cheeks. She was a physical and emotional wreck, but her troubles had only just begun. The missionaries couldn't have picked a worse time to try to convert the villagers. About one hundred and fifty highlanders were celebrating the opening of Peta's new cookhouse, and most of them were drinking whisky and rum they'd bought in Luganville.

When Gramma saw the missionaries he shook his head in disgust, and Ravu and the rest of the outraged highlanders shook their fists and bows and machetes at the *disales* who were disturbing the ritual to open the cookhouse. Everyone started chanting, *"Killem! Killem! Killem finis!"* ("Beat them! Beat them! Kill them!")

The taunts grew louder and more hostile as the angry warriors worked themselves into a frenzy. When several men screamed above the chanting crowd that they were going to kill and cannibalise the missionaries and feed their bones to the dogs, the panic-stricken woman fainted. Her skinny male companion started crying and pissed himself. Then while he hunched over and held his shaking legs, he was so afraid he shit himself as well. Man bush admires courage and someone that never shows weakness.

Gramma was disgusted when he saw so much blatant panic and terror. The woman stood up, and then the three clerics begged not to be killed. The light was fading when the blubbering woman pleaded for shelter and said she was about to die from exhaustion. Gramma replied, "That would be good. It will save us killing you and will give the dogs something to eat." He meant every word, and while he told them to go sleep in the jungle with the devils, the death threats that were being shouted by the furious crowd reduced the missionaries to blithering wrecks.

Gramma and Peta decided to let them live and allowed them to stay in the "*haos blong kava*" (a hut used to dry *kava*) about thirty metres from the *nakamal*. Then Gramma gave them some roasted taro and warned if they were still around in the morning, it would be the last time they watched the sun rise. They listened to taunts, threats, and blood-curdling screams, throughout what must have been a long and terrifying night. As soon as dawn cast enough light they fled down the trail to the lowlands.

About halfway through the journey inland, when Ravu asked where the gifts were, my reply of "What gifts?" stunned him. Especially when he had to explain they were to reciprocate the *essengo* rite I'd performed with Peta. He probably figured I'd remember the *essengo* I'd performed with him as well, but because I still had a memory like a sieve, I didn't. I'd mentioned the rituals in my notes, but they were different ceremonies from the one I'd performed with Ravae, and had different *tabus*, so it was an easy mistake to have made. I knew I'd probably be killed for such a serious breach of *kastom* so I banged on the roof of the pickup so that I could jump off and start walking back to Luganville. When we stopped Ravu said, "*Yumi* brothers, Tavua. No problem" ("We're brothers, Tavua. No problem").

In Middle Bush, if a man doesn't keep his word it can cost him his life. To someone with a Western mindset, simply being a *kastom* brother is hardly a persuasive argument for taking such a dangerous risk, but in the highlands, that kinship means everything. I trusted Ravu's judgement and valued his opinion, and although he said he couldn't speak for Peta, he felt that if I told Peta I would give him cash or send the gifts up to Nukurekum when I returned to civilization, I should be ok.

The next day, when we were about to enter Nukurekum, Ravu looked worried. Peta had regained his muscular physique and cheerful nature, but when he realized I'd arrived without any gifts, his warm welcome ended abruptly. A deadly hush fell over the hut. Vetrivu sneered and spat and then looked away. Voemanu also spat in disgust, as if to get rid of the bad taste I left in her mouth, then she turned her back on me because I'd disgraced my clan and my *kastom* family. Gramma glared at me and shook his head in disapproval, then

he quietly spoke to Peta in his native tongue. Ravu remained stoic and silent. When Peta reached for his bow and a barbed arrow there wasn't any hatred in his eyes. He was about to shoot me simply because it's *kastom*.
I looked Peta in the eyes and hoped he'd wound an arm or a leg, instead of keeping his bow aimed at my face. Even when the arrow sliced into my flesh, I wanted to take the pain like Peta's *kastom* son and brother would, instead of acting like a terrified *disale*. Gramma saved me from being seriously injured or killed when he moved between us and calmly suggested that because I was Peta's son, maybe I could give him cash instead of the gifts. When Peta grimly agreed I was stunned. A year ago he would've shot me without hesitation, but now the church had influenced his thinking.
I apologised and went outside to shake off my jangled nerves, and several minutes later, when I went back inside the hut was empty. I spent the first night back in Middle Bush alone.

Early the next morning, Ravae paid me a visit and said that last year, after he drank several shells of *kava* and entered a deep trance, the spirits had told him to sleep because Tavua was dying. During a vivid dream, he saw me battling for my life in a hospital bed and knew I'd die without his help. When he woke up he ran through the jungle to the *tabu* cave filled with ancestral skulls and asked all of the spirits to heal me. I was dumbfounded. There was no other way that Ravae could have known I had malaria because I hadn't told anyone on Santo about my illness.

Life is always unpredictable, and everything is taken at face value in Middle Bush. There's no place for ifs, buts, or maybes. Timid actions and absent-minded decisions don't belong. It had taken a long time to build a strong rapport with my *kastom* family and more importantly to gain their respect. By failing to reciprocate the *essengo*, I'd unwittingly destroyed years of hard work. My family were ashamed of me, because I was a man who'd shunned our values and had shunned being Peta's soul mate. I had to do some serious damage control, and as quickly as possible.

My first priority was to find Gramma and mend our friendship. I found him after a long search, and when he finished venting his anger I explained my memory loss. Then I dealt my ace card and told him I'd gotten the medicines for his aid post illegally when the New Zealand health authorities had refused to supply them to someone who wasn't qualified to handle prescription medicines. When I asked Gramma if he would risk being imprisoned in a foreign country to help *disales* who had threatened to kill him, his apologetic expression and the sympathetic tone of his voice when he said, "*Tavua kevoro*" ("Tavua let's go"), answered my question.

No one had returned to Nukurekum, and from what they'd taken, it looked like they were planning to stay away for a few days. I followed Gramma through several villages, then we crossed a valley and climbed up to a scruffy leaf hut nestled beside one of Peta's gardens. We went inside, and when Gramma explained my illness to a group of villagers and told them I'd provided the medicines at great personal risk, a look of remorse spread across everyone's face.

They rose to their feet and started saying, "*Tamamasa*, Tavua. *Tamamasa*." ("Everything is good, Tavua. Everything is good.") When Peta apologised to me his emotions were so sincere and so intense, it felt like I could reach out and physically touch them. I hoped Busa would be as forgiving as Peta was when I gave him 5,000 vatu as the gift for the *essengo*. One of the most important things I'd learnt was never to say no, I won't, I can't, or you can't. By explaining why a request wasn't possible, or why I hadn't done something, rather than bluntly saying no first, I gained respect. To do a good deed without emphasising how others would benefit from your actions also earns respect. Because I'd provided the medicines without mentioning the risks I'd taken, and because I was prepared to take my punishment without using my memory loss as an excuse, I was forgiven.

When we all hiked back to Nukurekum, Peta took me aside and said a week from now we would hunt wild bullock so that I could enjoy fresh meat. The day after the hunt, he'd kill his finest fowl, give me a mat, and prepare a feast for a *tamamasa* ceremony in my honour. Then he'd tell the villagers to perform a *kimpeti* dance for me. Although these showed me the utmost respect, I knew that when Peta didn't shoot me with his bow and draw blood for the spirits, they would demand another type of compensation, which is exactly what happened.

The next day, when Ravu asked me to go bow fishing I jumped at the chance to relax in the jungle with him. When we were about halfway from the stretch of river we were going to hunt, I veered off the trail while he jogged along a track below me. I yelled out in a gruff voice "Hey *Damate*," then when I jokingly drew a bead on him with a bow, he laughed and mimicked shooting back while he screamed a bloodcurdling war cry.

Towards the end of an enjoyable day, the next time he pointed an arrow at me he wasn't joking. While we were roasting a few fish and *tarovit* over a blazing fire, for no apparent reason the relaxed atmosphere suddenly turned hostile. Ravu looked ready to explode, then he picked up an arrow and flew into a rage. He thrust the barbed arrowhead to within millimetres of my eyes and said, "*Busa said it is up to me if I kill you, Tavua!!*" When he asked why I hadn't paid him 5,000 vatu as a gift for his *essengo* rite, like I'd done with Peta,

Ravu Magic with a fish he arrowed, just before he threatened to kill Rick.

I told him I couldn't remember anything about it. Because of his brutal reputation as a *matia*, I knew he wouldn't hesitate to kill me, and was stunned when he said, "*Tavua, fashion blong bubu rabis.*" ("Tavua, the way my ancestors think isn't good.") Even his unshakable faith in *kastom* had been affected by Christianity. He said I was a *kastom* brother, and an incredibly lucky one, because a year earlier, when he knew nothing about Sari (Jesus), he definitely would've killed me to please *Taute* and the sprits.

The next few days were also harsh. I thought Garae was going to hack me up with his machete, I got pinkeye, I slipped on a rock and split my head open, and when we pulled *kava* deep in the mountains I was given a ridiculously heavy load of the roots to carry. I was constantly being tested.

Over the next relaxing week there weren't any more anxious moments. I felt a huge sense of relief when Busa passed through the village and left my manhood intact. For someone who'd threatened me with extinction in the past, his verbal reprimand over failing to reciprocate the *essengos* was fairly tame.

Gramma, spear at the ready, stalking with deadly silent footfalls.

My gut feeling that he would definitely punish me proved to be right, when not long after he left us, the whole village became unfriendly. Peta warned me to sleep well, because in the morning, we were going down to the lowlands to hunt wild bullock with a spear. Then when I returned, I would visit Winea.

We were up at daybreak, and raced through the jungle at a reckless pace. When we stopped to chew and drink *kava* it provided a welcome rest until our journey started to resemble a pub crawl. After four drink stops where I was given eight bamboo cups filled with kava, I wasn't completely hammered, but I was well on the way. I knew I was being made to run the gauntlet, and accepted each drink Peta thrust into my hands without question. The recent rain had turned the Jordan River into such a fierce surge, I questioned my sanity to even think about crossing it, but when Gramma said, "No problem," I literally went with the flow, like man bush does with all of nature. After we'd crossed the river more times than we needed to, we climbed up to a plateau, where Gramma and Peta expertly stalked to within striking distance and speared a good-sized bullock.

That night, we made crude but comfortable beds by covering *lap lap* leaves with a thick mattress of *oauk* branches. Then we ate a few ribs and bits of offal that we roasted in the fires blazing alongside our beds. When we drank huge amounts of *kava* to toast our successful hunt, Peta kept filling our empty bamboo cups until we were both so drunk we vomited.

The next morning, I faked a smile and had to suppress the urge to throw up when Peta kept enforcing my punishment by bombarding my hungover system with more *kava*. After we shouldered heavy loads of meat and started the long hard climb up to the highlands, we kept stopping along the trail to drink more *kava*. By the time we'd reached the bottom of the steep climb up to Nukurekum, my resilience had been pushed to its absolute limits. Every fibre in my body felt so shattered I wanted to collapse on the side of the trail, curl up, and go to sleep.

Things went from bad to worse when Busa was conveniently sitting on the edge of a swollen stream at the base of the climb. He was drinking *kava* so the sprits would help him decide how severe my punishment should be. He grabbed his machete and waved it in my face while he threatened to kill and eat me, then he put his head down and sucked in a short breath just before a huge arc of vomit gushed from his mouth. Several minutes later, after an uncomfortable silence, I was given two more shells of *kava* that were so strong my already hazy vision almost doubled.

When it started to rain, and when Peta started moaning about his aching back and shoulders, it was obvious the opportunity to regain everyone's respect was being handed to me, as he never complains about anything. I picked up his heavy load, placed mine on my other shoulder, and started climbing up to the village.
While I slogged upwards in a drunken swagger, each one of my laborious steps felt like it was pumping battery acid through my aching muscles. My body begged me to stop, but I kept going, and staggered into the village ahead of everyone else.

As I entered our hut, Voemanu's eyes widened, she shook her head to express her disbelief, and then she shrieked "*Weeeee*!" when I asked where she wanted me to dump the meat.
While I was still gasping for breath, I breathed life back into a fire smouldering alongside my sleeping mat and warmed my shivering body.

Young boys carrying the spoils of the hunt.

Busa performing the *tuvetuveseri* rite.

Half an hour later, Busa squatted beside me and held his outstretched hands towards the flames. He looked at the massive bruises that were starting to appear on my shoulders, smiled, and then his one word, "Surprised," said it all. The stain had been removed from my respectability, but I felt too weak and sick to bask in the afterglow of having gained total acceptance again.

I still thrived on the challenge of pushing my resilience to its absolute limits and coping with uncertainty, but the following day, I was forced to become something I absolutely loathe when I took another step towards becoming a true man bush.

Rough Justice

Busa rewarded the exhausting way that I'd regained everyone's respect by inviting me to watch a rarely practised divination rite called *tuvetuveseri*. He performed the ritual on the *nasara*, and used ash, charcoal, stones from a cooking fire, short stakes of wild cane, and wild *kava* and yam leaves. After he'd finished the first part of the rite, he looked to the heavens and quietly chanted to *Taute* and the spirits. Half an hour later, when an eagle that was gliding on the thermals wheeled directly over our heads, Busa came out of a deep trance and announced who was responsible for breaking a *tabu* that was creating problems in our village.

After we finished watching the ritual, instead of working in the gardens with everyone else, Gramma said I should give my jaded body a rest, so we stayed in the village and cooked ourselves a tasty meal of beef and *kumala*. Just as we were about to start eating, the dogs snarled and barked a warning. Two natives were walking towards our hut. One of them was from another island, but because he was with a highlander who had moved to the lowlands, we thought nothing of it. Things started to go horribly wrong when the highlander went into the jungle to go to the toilet, and the visitor walked past the dogs and put his foot over our doorway. A stranger can't enter a hut unless he is asked to, and to walk inside a hut that's also a *nakamal* is so sacrilege, the spirits must be avenged with violence. When Gramma looked towards his bow I expected blood to flow, but he changed his mind and decided to overlook the honest mistake.

I gave our guests some food while Gramma started chewing *kava* for a welcome ceremony. The name of the native who barged into the hut was Kapie. He looked to be in his mid-twenties and was likeable and carefree, but his lively personality literally proved to be his downfall when he jokingly said that chewing *kava* was, "*Fashion blong pig.*" ("The fashion of a pig.") Gramma turned to me and said in a venomous tone, "*Killem Damate!*" ("Kill the devil!") To Gramma, Kapie's scathing remark had come straight from the mouth of a devil, and even worse, from someone who disrespected our beliefs.

As soon as I started to move Kapie's friend leapt to his feet and raced out the door. He knew what was about to happen, and that because he'd brought Kapie to our village he was responsible and would receive the same terrible punishment. I was the first to avenge our spirits. When Kapie slowly stood up, his look of bewilderment turned into a grimace when I flew through the air and slammed a vicious front kick into his temple.

I'm addicted to breathing, and knew I'd receive the same brutal treatment if I didn't fight, so I made sure plenty of blood flowed when we launched into a brutal frenzy of ruthless kicks and punches. I knew that bones must break, so I reached down, grabbed Kapie's hand, and snapped one of his fingers. Then as we landed another flurry of bone-crunching blows Gramma yelled,

"Killem, Tavua! Killem!" Taute needed more vengeance, so I nudged Gramma aside, lined up our victim's thigh, and delivered a loud kick. Gramma muttered a string of obscenities, and then he leapt in the air and stomped on Kapie's outstretched arm so hard that when it broke I heard a loud snap.

I felt relieved when the assault ended and Kapie's screaming trailed off to a series of groans. He started whimpering like a wounded animal and could barely move as he crawled towards the door, so we grabbed a leg each and dragged his quivering body to the edge of the village. Then Gramma kicked him in the head and said the highlander that had brought him here was going to get a worse beating the next time we saw him. Kapi was semi-conscious and looked more dead than alive. The pain must have been unbearable when we lifted him by his injured arms and legs and threw him down the slope at the village entrance. From the sound of his loud screaming as he rolled down the hill, it obviously was. We yelled obscenities at him and shouted that he belonged in the jungle with the devils, then we walked back inside as if nothing had happened and finished eating our lunch.

The assault made me realize how incredibly lucky I'd been in the past during tense situations that had the potential to become violent. It also made me realize Christianity still had a long way to go before it had an impact on everyone. When I wondered if Kapie would survive I had to divorce myself from feeling guilty or ashamed. We'd simply performed a violent ritual to ensure others respected our values and our protocol. The assault wasn't personal. It was brazen tribal justice, where the victim's feelings are never considered.

That afternoon, when Busa passed through our village to head down to the lowlands, he said my trip to Winea would have to wait until he returned, so Peta rescheduled the *tamamasa* ceremony for one week's time. As each day passed, the sickening stench of rotting beef began to fill our hut, and as usual, it didn't take long for the stomach-churning meals to ruin my health.

Now that Gramma knew I had the true fighting spirit of a man bush, our inseparable kinship grew even stronger. One afternoon, we walked for ten minutes from Nukurekum, and after he checked to make sure we were alone, he parted the overgrown vegetation surrounding the base of a *namele* palm. Then he pulled out an almost rectangular stone that had been shaped millennia ago by an ancient chief called Molilelei. The stone is called Sulevous, which means "the stone that is used for *kava*," and is used when a man with a huge amount of *rapee* is made a chief, so that he becomes empowered with the spirit of Molilelei and every other chief that has used the stone. Gramma, Peta, and Busa are the only living men that have ever seen or used the Sulevous. If any other highlander even looks at it they must be killed.

Gramma said I was allowed to see the sacred object because I was being prepared for something truly special that would provide the answers I was looking for.

Sulevous, the stone that is so sacred, if a highlander looks at it they must be killed.

I knew that if I was going to become a chief, it would require a lot of hard work, as it's like having a massive mortgage in a civilized society, especially if the sacred stone is used. An aspiring chief must rear ten pigs with curved tusks, and provide the food for a huge feast. Peta and Busa had more than three hundred hungry mouths to feed. Huge amounts of *kava* flow, and mountains of food are eaten during a celebration that normally lasts a week. *Kastom* forbids a chief to purchase his sacrificial pigs with money. This stops anyone who doesn't have the respect or the full support of the villagers from buying their leadership. A man can only become a patriarch by having a huge debt that will take years to pay back to his bloodline when they loan him extra pigs, supply the crops, and provide the labour for the feast. In the past, a chief sometimes sacrificed as many as twenty pigs, and in the distant past, a human was also sacrificed.

On the morning that Peta started preparing a *tamamasa* ceremony our hut was a hive of activity. Busy groups of women lit the cooking fires and got massive piles of taro and vegetables and other food ready. At midday, when everything was cooked, I grabbed a long wooden club and helped Ravu and Peta pound piles of steaming taro on a large wooden

Making nalot.

plate. Turning the taro into a tasty dough called *nalot* is part of an important and energetic ritual. We worked ourselves into a frenzy that became so intense, sweat coursed down our bodies and dripped into the steaming taro. While Ravu and I stopped to rest our aching muscles, Peta pounded out a pulsating tune called the *kore*, to tell everyone the feast and the ceremony were about to start.

When everyone was seated in the *nakamal*, the drone of chatter suddenly went silent when Peta walked to the centre of the floor. He made an emotional speech that said from now on all of his material possessions belonged to both of us, and any burdens or problems that we faced in the future were also ours.

The crowd were visibly moved when he said he would die to save my life during a battle, and that he'd sacrificed his most valuable rooster for the feast to show he had the greatest respect for me. After he gave me a mat, which is one of the biggest honours a man can receive during a *tamamasa* ceremony, I reciprocated by telling him my worldly possessions were also his and added it would be an honour to travel to the spirit world if I sacrificed my life during a battle for a brother with such powerful *rapee*. We shared a shell of *kava*, then I did the same with five other chiefs, which gave me an inseparable bond with all of them, and lifted my status to a height that should have been way beyond the reach of an adopted *disale*.

Once the formalities were over we ate huge amounts of food and drank shell after shell of *kava*. Then we sang and danced all night to the persistent rhythm of the *tam tams* and to the hollow sound of *bolo* sticks (one-metre-long portions of bamboo) pounding the ground. At four in the morning, I finally collapsed in an exhausted heap on my sleeping mat and snatched a few hours sleep before the *kimpeti* dance started.

It felt like I'd just drifted off to sleep when Peta shook me awake and told me to put on a *mul mul* and to wait on the *nasara*. An hour later he slowly walked down the steep slope from Vanakanakarea with a group of energetic dancers who twirled and shouted and stomped their feet. As they got closer, Peta sang an emotional chant that said I would always have a special place in his heart. The lively dancers were an impressive sight. The men wore *tabu* leaves and were painted with streaks of orange pigment from the *ol* nut, and most of the women had purple flowers tucked behind their ears.

When they reached the *nasara* the men formed a circle, then started singing, and pounded the earth in perfect unison with two-metre-long *lauma* sticks (bamboo dance sticks) while a swirling throng of women and children circled around them. We danced for hours in the humid heat until a thick sheen of sweat dripped from our bodies, and whenever we briefly rested to catch our breath, a chief from another village pounded the ground with a large piece of *wiaer* tree and sang a haunting melody.

Peta sacrificing one of his finest fowl for Rick's tamamasa ceremony.

At about two o'clock in the afternoon, Peta led us to the *nakamal* for a *kava* ceremony that became another mammoth drinking session. Around two o'clock the next morning, I collapsed onto my sleeping mat in a drunken, exhausted heap, while the others carried on drinking until dawn.

Whenever I lived in Middle Bush my body always went through a vicious cycle of arriving there healthy and having to leave when I'd become a physical wreck. The hard living and eating rotten meat for weeks had ruined my health. My complexion had turned yellow and my eyes were dull and discoloured, so I went to Luganville to get treated, but I was so unwell I decided to return to New Zealand.

Young boys swirling in a circle during the kimpeti dance.

Pounding out a hypnotic tune during the kimpeti dance.

Living On The Edge Of Life And Death

Almost a year passed before I was able to return to Middle Bush, and during that time the highlanders had been subjected to more change. Their timeless world had been rushed through the ages so they could learn about the white man's spirituality and morals. The desire to experience a better way of life that the Church promised had been so appealing to about a dozen of the one hundred and twenty highlanders, they'd shifted down to the lowlands.

When I climbed up to Nukurekum the Church's attempts to modernise the village seemed to have peaked without any real impact. Apart from a volleyball court outside our hut, the surroundings were still extremely primitive.

During my first Sunday morning back in Middle Bush, a bell rang at Vanakanakarea to call everyone to church. About twenty Christians filled the hut, and while I sat next to Ravu, he told me the strain of living in constant fear had been too much for the Protestant preacher who normally gave the service. He was leaving at the end of the year and had told his superiors that no other missionaries should be sent to Middle Bush. I wasn't surprised to see he was in the lowlands and having a break from his challenging job, but I was shocked to see Atison nervously standing at the pulpit and wearing a Protestant uniform. When he started preaching he kept wringing his hands and coughed nervously as he struggled to read from a Protestant bible written in Bislama.

While I listened to the sermon I could see why some of the highlanders had become Christians. Both religions believe in the power of gods, spirits, sacred objects, sorcery, prayer, and devils. Man bush found it easy to relate to why God had allowed Jesus to be crucified. They believe the sacrificial blood of Jesus saving mankind is similar to the *matia* offering blood from a family member to maintain spiritual harmony. They likened the way Jesus arose from the dead to a *matia's* victim surviving for five days when their heart has been replaced with a green coconut. Once they started comparing the Bible to *kastom*, many of the beliefs, and more importantly, some of the place names were the same. Having the Jordan River flowing through Santo and then seeing pictures of its namesake in the Bible convinced some of the natives the island had been blessed by the *disale* god. So did a story that has been passed on to each generation since the middle of the nineteenth century, when a missionary twisted part of the bible to help convert the natives. He told them Noah built the ark on top of Mount Tambewassana, and after it rained for forty days and forty nights, when the ship floated past the highlands, Noah planted a *natangora* palm (sago palm) so that its leaves could be used to rethatch the huts when the flooding subsided. Nowadays, because of the story, the people of Supemalau village in South Santo believe a boat-shaped rock that's perched on top of a nearby mountain is Noah's ark. They climb up to it every day, to worship it, and to keep it free of weeds.

Atison's eyes shine with joy during a bobo rite.

After the service, while everyone milled around outside, I asked them how they felt about Christianity. Most of them were disillusioned by the compromises they'd made. They couldn't understand why the pastor took money from them when they were already destitute and struggling to pay off their pickup truck and why he let them walk past his hut without inviting them in to share food, like they always did, because they would never commit such a heinous breach of *kastom*. They couldn't understand the hypocrisy of a religion that condemned other Churches that worship the same god, and they asked why they were told an atheist would be damned to hell, when every highlander goes to *Taute's* heaven.

The Church created so much unrest and bitterness that it destroyed close friendships and almost started a war between two villages. But by far the worst thing that happened was when the *matia* went on a killing spree to nurture the devil with human sacrifices, so that he would be powerful and able to overwhelm the white man's god. Even the *matia* who went to church were using black magic and murdering and eating their victims to feed the devil. It was a dangerous time, where everyone lived on the edge of life and death.

Several days after my arrival, Garae was deep in the jungle cutting firewood when a wayward swing of his machete hacked into his foot. The razor-sharp blade sliced the underside of his big toe, from the tip to where the toenail begins. He stopped the bleeding with wild *kava* sap, and scraped *kava* bark into the wound to relieve the pain during his strenuous one-hour trek back to the village. When he hobbled into our hut he refused my offer to stitch the flap back together and gritted his teeth while Gramma rinsed the wound clean. Then he slit a chicken's throat, pulled the cut wide open, and poured the sacrificial blood into it. The three of us were going to Winea the next morning, and despite his injury, Garae told us not to leave without him.

We were up at dawn, and while we jogged through the steamy rainforest a plastic rice bag that I'd taped around Garae's heavily bandaged toe quickly filled with blood. The way he raced up the steep climb to Winea was typical of just how resilient man bush is. I felt fit and strong and had been running marathons in New Zealand, but I still couldn't keep up with him. At the halfway point, when he cut down some bamboo that was full of water and handed me a drink, as soon as the first rancid mouthful hit the bottom of my stomach I vomited.

Any other time I wouldn't have been overly concerned about catching an illness from the brackish water, but during our journey Gramma had told me I was about to face a ritual that's so brutal and so *tabu*, most villagers die. The rite is so intimidating and secretive, the villagers are afraid to even mention its name, *Mate Tanatau Maori*, which means, "dying to get the full power of life."

No one had told the two pygmy women I was coming. When I entered the village they stopped weaving their half-finished mats, screamed, and hurled them into the air. Then they sprang to their feet and sprinted into the nearest hut as fast as their stumpy little legs would carry them. Silas and Matai ran across the *nasara* to greet me and roared with laughter at the terrified women's response.

Atison nervously delivering a sermon.

After we'd finished a welcome ceremony with Busa, Silas rubbed his hand over my stubble and said if I didn't shave, in a month I'd be ready for a beard-cutting ceremony. When the first hair sprouts on an adolescent's chin he looks forward to growing a full beard, because the first time it's shaved is the most important moment in a male's life. The boy's uncle normally performs the ritual, and each time he cuts off a bit of beard, he trims feathers from a live fowl and snips bristle from a live pig until the boy is clean-shaven.

Then when the boy and the uncle give each other a mat it's the boy's proudest moment. He's just become a man and is ready to find a wife. Because it was agreed that I wouldn't get married to a highlander, my initiation into manhood was going to be a lot more brutal than having my beard cut, and was going to be a lot more traumatic than I could ever have imagined.

A tabu waterfall near the base of the climb up to Winea.

Peta and Ravu climbed up to Winea late in the afternoon, and that night, the rancid water had made me so sick I was lying on my sleeping mat with painful nausea and a high fever.

Ravu performed a healing and divination rite, then he said during my trip to Winea I drank brackish water because *Damate* had watched me and said, *"Himi who yea?"* ("Who is this?") The spirits had told Ravu the devil had poisoned me and that if he didn't exorcise *Damate* from my spirit I'd die.

Not long after midnight, I staggered outside and sensed the same supernatural presence that I felt during my last visit to Winea. I was way too sick to reach the nearby jungle, so I vomited and emptied my screaming bowels alongside the hut.

The next morning, when Peta stepped outside and saw an unusually thick mist and then said someone had died, everyone burst out laughing when I apologised for shitting so close to the hut, and I said I'd clean up the mess once I felt better. He wasn't referring to the smell. The mist was an omen that told him someone important had just died. Later, we received a message that a chief had suddenly died in the lowlands at the same time that the eerie-looking fog had rolled across to Winea.

The following day Matai gave me a rusty two-inch-long metal spike that one of his ancestors had received as payment for cutting sugarcane in Queensland for two years. Every child from each successive generation was shown it, told about the blackbirders, and warned to never trust the white man. When Matai handed me the spike he said, "We want you to have this because like our ancestor you have been through years of pain for what might have seemed like a small payment. Your time has come, Tavua. You must stay strong my brother. If you survive what you must face, you'll be a special man."

That night and the following week were easily the hardest days of my life. I'm not going to explain what I went through just yet. I'll give you an in-depth explanation about how I survived the ritual a second time when I returned to Winea years later.

After I completed the rite I could barely walk when I staggered back to Nukurekum. I didn't think the human body could survive so much terrible abuse, and wondered how much more punishment mine could take. I felt so exhausted and so unwell that I decided to head back to New Zealand to recover. Garae's toe had become a puss-filed mess that needed treatment so he joined the other villagers who came with me to Luganville.

I left myself just enough money to travel back to New Zealand and spent the rest on medicines and other essential goods for the villagers. Later in the day, while I was resting at John Noel's, Busa and Ravu visited me because they were worried I'd used most of my money. They gave me some food, and said they were sorry for "spoiling me."
Then they showed me the deepest respect when they crossed their arms and pulled them tightly into their chests and said "*Tamamasa, Tavua.*" The simple gesture has immense meaning in Middle Bush. It signified that the spirit of our friendship would always be in their hearts. That special moment will stick with me forever. It was a fitting way to say goodbye to Busa, because sadly, it was the last time I ever saw him.

Matai, dwarfed by his bow.

Spiritual Mayhem

Whenever I travel I never have any expectations, which is just as well, because my next trip to Santo wasn't very productive. Earlier in the year, a hurricane carved a destructive path through the highlands and left a mass of destroyed property and ruined gardens in its wake. It also caused spiritual mayhem. Busa was on the brink of death, and some of the highlanders were adamant that *Damate* had wreaked havoc on Middle Bush because of Busa's weakening spirit.

He'd looked tired and unwell when we'd said our final goodbyes. His normally muscular stomach had become so smooth and bloated he looked pregnant. He died in his sleep in early May 2001, and so did four other men who were suffering from the same illness. They were all *matia* who had tried to feed the devil by drinking human blood as if it was water, and by eating more human hearts than anyone had ever done before. Everyone believes the *matia* died because they overloaded their bodies with massive amounts of spiritual power that no mortal could survive. Busa was the most powerful *matia* that ever lived, so he was always in danger of dying from too much *rapee* or from being killed by other *matia* who wanted to become empowered with his potent spirit.

When I heard about Busa's death while I was in Luganville, the terrible news dazed and saddened me. I also learned several highlanders had started a rumour that *Damate*, *Taute*, and all of the spirits had caused the spate of catastrophes because Tavua, a man who looked like a *disale*, had been given too much *tabu kastom*.
Then when another hurricane bombarded Middle Bush while everyone was still recovering from the previous cyclone, a ten-year-old boy died, and the highlanders' Toyota was washed away when a flash flood surged along the Jordan River. Living in Middle Bush was never easy at the best of times. After I was warned the villagers who started the rumour would probably try to poison or kill me, I decided not to head up to Nukurekum. My presence would've created more unwelcome problems at a time when everyone was busy trying to rebuild their lives.

Only a week after I arrived in Vanuatu, I flew back to Port Vila and became infected with a water-borne parasite called giardiasis. Although it's a deadly disease, I had to laugh at how ironic it was to have caught it in a suburb called Freshwater. When I returned to New Zealand, as the plane took off and climbed above a layer of thin white cloud, I gazed across the horizon towards Santo and thought about Busa. When pygmies were first discovered they were named after the Greek word pygme, which is a measurement that translates to, "half an arm's length." The impact Busa's death had on the highlands is immeasurable. He left a massive void in a people who are on the verge of extinction, as there are now only four men and two women that are true pygmies.

Rick with Busa, the last great pygmy chief.

From a *disale* point of view, I'd lost the race against time to document everything there was to know about the last great pygmy chief, but when I thought like a man bush, Busa is with *Taute* and the spirits, in an eternal world where time never runs out.

Time no longer stood still in the highlands. It was restless and anxious as it ticked into an uncertain era. I felt a real sense of urgency to return and document as much as I could before man bush ended up like other tribes I'd lived with that became detribalised, dehumanised misfits that didn't feel comfortable in either a primitive or modern society.

When Natural History New Zealand and National Geographic Television asked me to film a documentary in Middle Bush, I sent a message to the chiefs that asked for the people's permission. They welcomed the idea on the condition that I did the filming alone.
While I was returning to Vanuatu to finalize everything, someone started a rumour that a video camera stole a person's *rapee*, and even if they somehow managed to survive, their

body would mutate and they'd suffer horrific physical deformities. Then to make things worse, the lowlanders warned if a film crew passed through their territory to film me before I went up to the highlands, they would be greeted with violence.

When Gramma and I passed through their villages they treated me well and said that despite their harsh warning, I was always welcome. But before we climbed up to Nukurekum, we received a message that up in the mountains, the villagers had become so divided over the documentary, if it went ahead there would be bloodshed and I'd be the first to die. Although I made it known I had no intentions of going ahead with the documentary, when we entered Nukurekum the tense atmosphere was filled with uncertainty.

Peta had become the new paramount chief, but my alliance with him didn't make me immune to an attack from another villager. That night, when I became violently ill after a welcome ceremony, I couldn't help but wonder if someone had poisoned me.

The next morning, I woke up with a headache, but I made an instant recovery when Peta offered to treat me with a miniature bow and a small arrow tipped with a shard of glass. The last time he'd used it on Vetrivu she nearly died when he shot the "*rope*" (vein) on her temple to bleed out the "*Rabis blud*" (dirty blood) and severed the artery that was carrying evil spirits to her head. Each beat of her racing heart spurted frightening arcs of blood into the air, and when she fainted, everyone thought *Damate* had claimed another victim until Peta revived her with cold water.

Over the next few weeks, I kept filling my notebooks with *kastom* until one evening Peta and Gramma said there was nothing else for me to write about. Gramma reached over and held my arm, then he said, "Tavua, teaching you our *kastom* has been hard. Sometimes my heart felt heavy because it's not easy for us to share our

Because of intermarriage with taller clans, Busa's son, Sakele, (pictured with his own son,) towers over his father.

beliefs, but in my mind I know our *kastom* is nearly finished. I want my son and his son to know how we lived. You have been through much pain, but now you are a true man bush. Peta and I are going to give you the highest honour a man can receive. It beats everything. Tomorrow we will go to the jungle. I will make you a bow and a poisoned arrow."

The next morning, while we climbed to the top of Mount Reosara, way below us, a huge white water tank looked like a festering pimple on the face of the beautiful rainforest. Gramma had helped three men haul the plastic tank up from the lowlands so that the Christians at Vanakanakarea had a handy supply of water. He looked at it, shook his head from side to side in disapproval, and then said, "I helped carry that up the mountains. It is good small. That's the *disale* way. Man bush enjoys walking through the jungle to gather fresh water. The *disale* must beat nature and bring the water to him."

We climbed a carpet of gnarled roots, reached the summit, and dropped down the other side into open jungle, where Gramma pointed to a tree with a girth about the same as a man's forearm. Because my totem is the flying fox and the bow was to be purely ceremonial, the stave had to come from a *tule garae* tree. Although the *wuluwulu garae* palm was the true mother of the flying fox clan, the *tule garae* also helped to create the flying fox bloodline. The trunk was straight, free of disease and knots, and looked like a good choice.

Gramma slowly rubbed his hands over the bark, then instead of hacking into the tree, he treated the gift from *Taute* with the utmost respect. Each swing of his machete sliced into the wood with the care and passion of an artist that was about to transform one of *Taute's* creations into a work of art. Once he'd decided which side of the stave would be the back and belly, he patiently whittled it in half lengthwise. It's *tabu* for women to see a bow until it's finished, so he wrapped it in *lap lap* leaves before we headed back to Nukurekum.

In the past, a bowyer never rushed making a bow. It took about a month to carve the stave with a crude stone axe, and then the limbs were scraped with a sharpened pig tusk and rubbed smooth with a piece of fine coral or a block of sandstone. Nowadays it takes about an hour with a machete and a rasp. Most highlanders prefer to use green timber because it's much easier to work with, but there are a few who season a stave in the firewood rack above the cooking fire.

When Gramma started chopping with his machete, as the bow grew in his hands, each cut was different. Some were made visually by reading the timber, while others were made by feeling and following the flow of the grain. When he was almost ready to see if the limbs flexed properly, he shook his head because of a tiny pin knot that he hadn't been able to remove.

He stopped for a break, and when we returned I could see he was deeply disappointed that someone had burnt the shavings and woodchips from the bow. This breach of *tabu* had disrupted the harmony between Gramma and the spirits. *Taute* had already decided the bow's fate. I knew Gramma was upset because the bow was an extension of his spirit, and embodied with his *rapee*, and now he knew I would never be able to take it back to New Zealand. He became lost in his work again, and once he'd finished, I could feel his apprehension and watched him grimace when he cautiously bent the limbs until there was a loud and sudden snap. I would've cherished the bow, but I simply smiled at Gramma and told him worse things have happened. If the bow had survived, it would've been stored in the rafters so the smoke from our cooking fires would slowly season the timber and stain it a beautiful dark colour.

Gramma straightening an arrow shaft.

Then when I fired the first shot from it I would've tried to kill an animal so I could rub its blood into the bow and empower it with *rapee*. If the arrow missed, the bow would've been spiritually dead, and ended up as firewood. Two out of three new bows break, so a weapon that secures a kill with its first shot and then lasts and shoots well is a precious item.

We went inside the hut and Gramma pulled a piece of dried wild cane from the rafters, then he locked the doors to keep out the women, and started making my poisoned arrow.

The sacred arrows, called *Patevina*, are used to kill man. They are considered so dangerous and so *tabu*, none are kept in the villages. The few that do exist are stored in a well-hidden cave.

After Gramma pulled the wild cane across glowing embers and applied pressure to straighten the shaft, he inserted three barbed arrowheads made from black palm. Then he tied two chicken feathers to the shaft so they were on opposite sides and just below the arrowhead.

He chose one black and one white feather, to signify the brotherhood between himself, the ebony man bush, and Tavua, the white man bush.

When he'd finished he said, "Himi spirit blong yumi, Tavua" ("This is our spirits joined together, Tavua"). The arrow was finished physically, but it was far from complete. He wrapped it in *lap lap* leaves and gave it to Peta.

The next day, Peta left at dawn with the arrow, and returned at dusk after he'd jogged through the mountains to the *tabu* cave filled with ancestral skulls.

Peta is the only one with enough *rapee* to perform the rite that makes *Patevina* deadly poisonous. He sang to the skulls for over an hour and chanted into a *tabu oktre* leaf. Then while he was in a deep trance, he crushed the leaf and milked its juice along the arrow to empower it with *Taute's* spirit.

That night, when Peta was about to give me *Patevina*, he said to treat it with the greatest care and respect. If I used it to kill an enemy, as it flew through the air I'd hear *Taute* singing from the two feathers. This would help me find it, as I was to do everything that was humanly possible to retrieve such a sacred and dangerous object. If the arrowhead pricked my skin and drew blood I'd suffer a terrible death when *Taute* invaded my soul. This was the ultimate gift that I could receive from a mortal and was like so many other parts of *kastom* that were full of contradictions. It gave me immense life force, but if I made the slightest mistake with it, I'd die.

Patevina, the deadly arrow that's used to kill man.

Peta lifted *Patevina* above his head, and while he looked up at the arrow he said in a reverent tone, "*Taute*, empower *Patevina* for Tavua. If any man tries to kill Tavua, when he enters battle he will be fearless, he will be deadly accurate, and *Patevina* will kill our enemies without mercy. *Taute*, when *Patevina* and Tavua leave us, the spirit of the flying fox will be with them."

After Peta handed me the arrow we ended the simple rite by sharing a shell of *kava*. Now that I'd received *Patevina*, to every man bush Tavua was much more than just a man. I possessed some of the most potent magic, and my spirit was filled with immense supernatural power.

The next morning, I decided to go to Luganville and then fly back to New Zealand. While Gramma and I headed to civilization, without saying anything, we had an intuitive understanding that I'd return and reach the end of the *kastom* road, but we both knew I had to wait a few years.
As we went our separate ways we never said goodbye. Gramma looked me in the eye and said, "It is hard, Tavua," then he put his head down and walked away.

Photographing the highlanders had been extremely difficult. Trying to safely film them was also a huge challenge.

The End Of The Kastom Road

Documenting the beliefs of man bush and other tribes in Vanuatu had demanded that I willingly abuse my body. Over the years, mine had taken a terrible beating from *kastom's* unforgiving flurry of punches, so I had a break from Vanuatu and kept working as a photo-journalist in the Solomon Islands. While I lived with a group of militants towards the end of the civil war, I was subjected to the same fears and threats that they faced. The first night after I left the Solomons, those terrible experiences exposed my own frightening level of instinct for self-preservation when I thought I was still under threat, and I almost snapped the neck of a close friend that I thought was trying to kill me.

While I was back in New Zealand I decided I needed a break from the negativity that came with my occupation. I tried to live an ordinary life, but I knew I had to finish my personal journey in Middle Bush, and I also wanted to film the highlanders' beliefs so they had a visual record of *kastom* before it was lost forever.

In March of 2005, I formed Hakatrak Productions and returned to Vanuatu. The chiefs welcomed my proposal, and after they called everyone together, they even agreed that I could return with a cameraman, which was a huge surprise. Then when I returned to New Zealand, for the next six months I fought my way through a web of bureaucratic red tape to try to get permission from the Vanuatu government. It wasn't easy, because the chiefs had warned me that if anyone from the Cultural Centre accompanied me, which was the government's policy, they would kill them. After a lot of correspondence, the regulations were changed so that the Sanma Provincial Council (Santo's provincial council) could nominate a cultural protector to accompany me while we filmed.

I knew I had to be incredibly fit to survive the *Mate Tanatau Maori* ritual a second time. Although I suffered from bouts of recurrent malaria, I still put myself through a punishing fitness routine and purposely put on a few kilos of fat to help keep me alive during the brutal rite. A New Zealand broadcaster, TV3, funded my expedition and planned to air it on 60 Minutes. I was in an unusual and unenviable situation. Because *Mate Tanatau Maori* is so *tabu*, I couldn't tell TV3 that I was about to face the ritual and that my chances of surviving it were slim.

On the 24th of August I flew to Vanuatu with a cameraman who doesn't want to be named, so I'll simply call him Cameraman. I'd always felt uncomfortable about taking a *disale* to Middle Bush, and knew that realistically the only safe way to film a documentary was by myself. I warned Cameraman that in the highlands I became Tavua, and if he broke a *tabu*, because I'd be taking him to Middle Bush, *kastom* demanded that I help to inflict his punishment.

Some of the villagers wore filthy clothing,
while others reverted back to their pagan beliefs.

Although he'd worked in war zones and was used to living off his wits, nothing could've prepared him for the contradictions of *kastom* and the mindset of man bush. Then I had to overcome another problem when I met Gramma in Luganville and he said some of the highlanders were threatening to kill the cultural protector the Sanma Provincial Council had chosen, so I arranged to use John Noel's twenty-three-year old son, George, instead. His great sense of humour and maturity and resilience made him a valuable asset to our expedition.

When we travelled inland we spent our first night in a village near the Jordan River. The chiefs had demanded we wear loincloths to show that we respected *kastom* and *Taute*, so I wore mine to get used to the chilly nights when I slept up in the mountains. The cold kept me awake until I had a hellish bout of malaria that made my teeth chatter so much I thought I was going to bite my tongue off. I had a terrible night, and only managed to get an hour's sleep, which was hardly the ideal start to our journey.

As we followed the Jordan River, when I saw pornographic graffiti scrawled across *tabu* rocks and I saw a few highlanders walking along the trail wearing clothes, I had a gut feeling that in the six months since my last visit huge changes had taken place. When we reached Nukurekum my instincts were right, but the changes were different from what I thought might have happened. About half of the villagers were wearing filthy clothing, the Protestant minister had left for good, the church and school had closed down, and most of the Christians had reverted back to their pagan beliefs.

Kastom had become so strong again that the *matia* were on another killing spree, and during a dispute one of our enemies was killed and eaten. The most noticeable change contradicted the highlanders' ethics and their return to *kastom*. Most of the teenage boys were swearing in English, and even Gramma's three-year-old son greeted me by saying, "*Disale* bastard." If he'd done that a year earlier he probably would've been whipped until blood flowed, but now, Gramma just laughed and shrugged his shoulders.
Other social and political changes had taken place during my absence. Peta had been attacked by black magic, and became so unwell he wasn't able to fulfil his chiefly duties, so Gramma was made the paramount chief.

The next morning, Gramma knew I had malaria, but he asked me to go down to the lowlands to help him carry a heavy load back up to the village. I was obviously being tested to make sure I still had the fighting spirit of a true man bush, and although it required a superhuman effort, we jogged down the mountains, picked up our loads, and climbed back up to Nukurekum. A few hours later Gramma took me aside and said, "You have a strong heart, Tavua. I'm proud to have you as a *kastom* brother. Tomorrow I'm going to do something that has never been done by our people. I'm going to give you the same powers as a paramount chief."

This gave me the right to film and share extremely *tabu kastom* with outsiders and also gave me the right to save Cameraman's life three times if he breached a serious *tabu*. It was just as well, because that afternoon, when he unwittingly broke a tribal law, under normal circumstances I would've had to kill him without hesitation or be killed myself. We were both in an unusual and grim situation. He was given permission to enter Middle Bush to serve a purpose, and if he didn't complete his task, and he tried to leave or the villagers could sense he was afraid, they would be like a pack of wild dogs and move in for the kill and rip him apart. He handled the situation well, but it made a daunting start to the most challenging month of my life.

We started filming the next day, when Gramma and I went inside the decaying remains of a hut and performed the extremely secretive rite to make me a paramount chief. Gramma made a tattooing tool with three long green thorns from a *mole* tree and a piece of wild cane. Then he burnt a piece of kauri gum and mixed the soot with the juice from a *raubosbos* leaf to make a dark pigment for the tattoos I was about to receive.

I'm not allowed to expose some of our beliefs and everything I've seen or taken part in, so unfortunately I can't explain the crux of what I experienced when I received four *bulu* tattoos on the upper part of my left arm. The circular tattoos were given to me for several reasons. They empowered me with Gramma and *Taute's rapee*, gave me a long life, sexual prowess (as part of the rite demands I get married), good health, and happiness. They also filled my spirit with love, inner peace and joy and ensured I'd be absolutely selfless and hospitable. They also ensured I'd strive to be the best human being that I can, but no matter how I tried, my character would still have its flaws, as man bush believes that is part of being truly human.

If the circumstances demanded it, from now on I must "stand up," which means fight to the death to protect our *kastom* and any highlander who is being threatened. It also made Gramma and I "*wan kind*" ("one kind" or "of the same blood"), which gave us a bond that surpasses the *essengo's* eternal kinship.

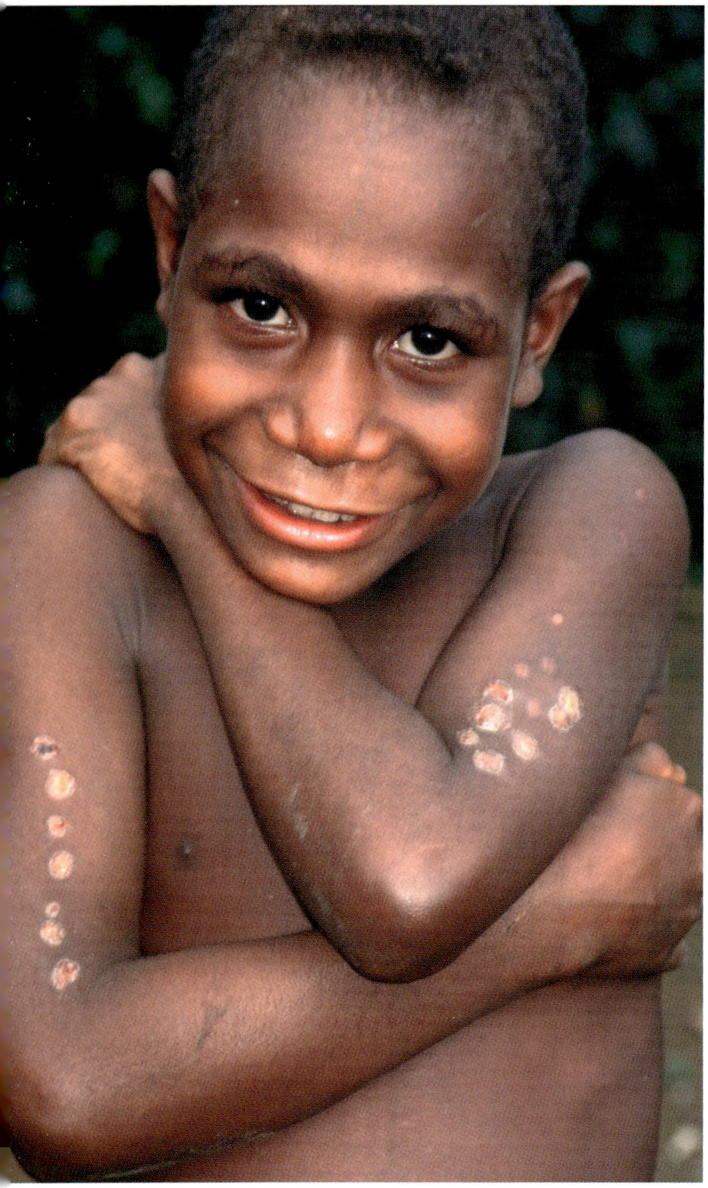

A young boy with healing bulu scars.

When Gramma finished the tattoos he pushed a piece of sago palm into the middle of the square my tattoos formed, and then lit it. As it seared into my flesh it created a *susulumachmach bulu*, which is extremely potent and protects me from *Damate* and evil spirits. Then he finished the simplistic rite by saying a reverent prayer to *Taute*.

After I'd patiently waited for nearly ten years, now I had the right to share sacred information that answered questions I'd been asked numerous times. When I was involved in public speaking in New Zealand, someone usually asked how I gained acceptance from a people who hate the white man, when I look like a European.

The reason I became Tavua began thousands of years ago, when man bush lived in another distant land, and began an amazing journey. The highlanders' dialect is *diale*, which means, "that person isn't here" or "he's gone somewhere else." This is very relevant to why I was accepted, because the highlanders' ancestors did actually go somewhere else, when they left Africa.

It required incredible courage to face the rigours of an epic ocean voyage where they relied upon hope, the guidance of their spirits, and their primitive navigation to try to discover a distant world that might not have existed. When a flotilla of about two hundred huge canoes caught the seasonal winds with sails woven from fibrous leaves, the primitive mariners survived on provisions they knew how to preserve and managed to elude the monsters and demons that they thought were waiting to attack them when they sailed beyond the horizon. They navigated by using the stars and planets, the flight paths of migratory birds, swell patterns, and cloud formations. Sometimes a naked sailor slipped into the ocean and used his testicles to feel the flow of the currents, to make sure they were following the right liquid path.

As the months passed, their food ran out and the long and hazardous voyage started to take its toll. When they started dying from thirst and hunger all they hoped for was a speedy death or that their prayers to sight land would be answered by the gods. After months of living in a claustrophobic canoe amidst a vast ocean, when a delirious sailor saw a cluster of dark clouds in the distance he mustered the last of his strength and climbed the top of the mast. The weeks of despair, the hallucinating from thirst and starvation, and the dreams they had about sighting a lush paradise were over when he saw the peaks of a rugged mountain range beneath the clouds. The ecstatic sailor shouted, "*Tu maori*" ("We are alive"), and when the canoes landed and some of the natives settled in a land that eventually became New Zealand, they were so grateful to be alive they called themselves *Maori*.

Then when some of them sailed north in search of a warmer, kinder climate, they eventually colonized parts of Vanuatu. This part of *kastom* fascinated me, because while I lived in the Solomon Islands with the primitive Kwaio they told me they evolved from Africa, and so did the peoples from Tongoa and Erromango islands in Vanuatu.

I'm a New Zealand *Maori* who belongs to the Tainui tribe. In the highlanders' language, *maori tuai* means "*kastom*" or "the life from the time before" or "the life of our ancestors." One of my *Maori* ancestors, my great-grandmother, was a revered tohunga (a priestess similar to a *kastom* woman) who was famous for her ability to mediate with the spirits. When I first walked across Santo and Ravae said I was Tavua, it was because man bush believes I was already one of them from the eternal link our ancestors have. The highlanders realize they are Melanesian and that New Zealand *Maoris* are Polynesian, and that the two cultures have many distinct differences. But just like man bush, there are *Maori* tribes that also believe they originated from different places around the world.

Blowing the tavue shell before a hunt.

Although I'd become a paramount chief, Gramma had the most political power and made any important decisions. When Cameraman had breached a serious *tabu* it created huge problems. For the first couple of days most of the villagers didn't want to be filmed, and Gramma refused to show him any other *tabu* rituals. We treated him with the utmost respect and offered him the very best of what we had, but he was lucky to be alive.
It was a dangerous time for everyone. During my previous visit, Gramma had warned me that the *matia's* killing had become rampant and said, "Our people are being murdered like sick chickens." Things were so bad that a close friend of mine, Agi, was hunted down and shot through the heart with a barbed arrow because he amassed an unacceptable tally of murders that defied his role as a *matia*.

When Cameraman made another unintentional breach of *kastom* that should've cost him his life, I saved him again. Peta decided to teach him respect and expand his thinking by using *kastom* to remove the sound from the footage we were shooting of everyone working in the garden.

Cameraman couldn't understand what was happening to his equipment until we told him what Peta had done. Then Peta allowed the camera to work again, and later, to reinforce how important it was for Cameraman to respect our *kastom*, we performed a ritual that gave him a tangible connection with the supernatural. The rite is practised in other parts of Vanuatu, but involves different ancestral spirits, and has been witnessed by thousands of people during cultural shows that were held in Port Vila.

Gramma cut a feathery shaped leaf that was about one and a half meters long from a *namele* palm. Then he placed the bulbous end in a shallow hole in the ground about 200 millimetres deep, refilled it, and gently compacted the soil around the base of the leaf. Cameraman is a big guy who weighs well over one hundred kilos, but no matter how hard he tried, when we told him to try to pull it out, his straining muscles couldn't match the incredible power of an unyielding spirit that held the leaf firmly in the ground.

The *namele* leaf is incredibly sacred to man bush. *Namele* means "man," and every *namele* palm in Middle Bush is empowered by the spirit of Taribo, an ancestral chief who is famous for sacrificing more than one thousand pigs. Whenever a *namele* leaf is placed in the ground it has the same *rapee* as all of the blood from Taribo's sacrificial pigs spilling onto the earth. On other islands in Vanuatu, when *nakaimas* have challenged me to pull out a *namele* leaf, they've used powdered human bone and other *kastom* to summon a spirit, but in Middle Bush we have such an intimate bond with the supernatural, and the spirit of Taribo is so incredibly powerful, that anyone with the ability can simply plant a leaf in the ground and it's impossible to remove it.

Whenever a pig is sacrificed a *namele* leaf is always brushed across its forehead, to release its spirit when it dies. Our welcome dance had been delayed because most of the villagers were livid that Cameraman had broken two *tabus.* When we gave him an official welcome, and we killed a sacred pig in our honour, Gramma refused to use the *namele* leaf. This had never been done before, and gave us some incredibly interesting footage for our documentary. The pig refused to die, even after I hit it so hard that I snapped a hardwood club. I hate seeing animals suffer, so I slit its throat, and although all of the blood drained from its body, fifteen minutes later it was still alive and clearly breathing because the *namele* leaf hadn't been used.

One of the many problems we faced with filming in such a remote location was having enough batteries for our camera. The solar panel we were given to power our battery charger didn't supply enough voltage, so Gramma said we would run down to the lowlands and use a generator. I knew it was part of the test to show that I was still worthy of facing *Mate Tanatau Maori* a second time and that the pain I was about to endure provided the spirits with restitution for when Cameraman had breached *kastom.*

It was a huge ask, because I'd suffered another bout of malaria, had undergone the draining and overwhelming effects of being empowered with Gramma's *rapee*, and I was being fed huge amounts of food, which symbolised me becoming a "big man" when I was made a paramount chief.

After we recharged the batteries, and after an exhausting run, when we arrived back at Nukurekum just on midday, which is what we'd told Peta, it was just as well. While we were away Cameraman had sat beneath a tree and read a book. This simple act was a scathing insult to our beliefs and to us. Any guest who comes to Middle Bush must try their best to mingle and be friendly. Man bush looks for humour in everything, and the highlands is a place to wallow in the joy and happiness of simply being alive and enjoying each other's company. It's not somewhere for a visitor to quietly read a book and to keep to himself instead of making an effort to form friendships with his hosts. Cameraman's attitude confused everyone. They thought he was being "high minded" (arrogant) or, even worse, some of them thought he was acting like a devil.

While Gramma and I were charging the batteries, Peta, Atison, Ravu, and most of the other young boys and men were getting ready to kill Cameraman. They'd given us until one o'clock to return and had decided that if we weren't back by then, they were going to cut off Cameraman's ear and feed it to him. Peta felt it would be the perfect payback for not taking heed of my warnings. Then they were going to kill him with their fists, *nul nul*s, machetes, knives, and bows. After everyone ate an equal portion of his heart and drank his blood, they were going to roast his body in the cooking stones. *Kastom* demanded that Gramma and I also drink some of the blood and eat part of the heart and that we join the others when they feasted on his flesh. Atison was really looking forward to eating Cameraman. When I filmed him later, he told me he'd recently shot one of our enemies in the thigh with a barbed arrow and was disappointed his terrified victim had escaped, as he was going to cannibalise him. When I asked him what Cameraman would've tasted like he said, "*Numba wan* (great), and sweet, like a pig."

The following days were a living nightmare. Human flesh has a very distinct smell when it's roasting in the cooking stones. When I had to use my chiefly right to save Cameraman for the last time, I also lost the right to tell him that if he insulted *kastom* again he would be cannibalised. Whenever I left him alone in the village, each time I returned I looked for the telltale smoke from a cooking fire seeping through the thatch roof, and I sniffed the air and hoped like hell I didn't smell *disale* fat and flesh being cooked. To have a foot firmly planted in each culture, and to have to try to save what was realistically an innocent man from daily beatings and from being killed, drew on all of my intellect, resolve, compassion, and understanding.

The mood became more and more tense as the villagers' simmering hatred of Cameraman grew stronger while we filmed everyday life and re-enactments of brutal rites. With the torment that my mind and body were going through, even simply existing in the primitive conditions would've been demanding. I had to draw on years of experience and had to reach into that special place we all possess, but very rarely have to use, to flush away all of the negativity and to brace myself for the *Mate Tanatau Maori* ritual, because to survive it twice, as I was about to do, is a rarity, and no one lives through it a third time.

Early one morning, I told Cameraman we were heading to Winea, and that I had to perform a ritual that I might not survive. It wasn't an easy thing for me to do under those circumstances, but Gramma had reassured me that if I died, he would make sure Cameraman got out of the highlands alive if he adhered to *kastom*. The harsh climb up to Winea taxed my already weary body, and that night, in the most *tabu nakamal* in Middle Bush, after I drank five shells of potent *kava*, they opened up a portal to a world that most people would find highly unreal. This supernatural realm is filled with incredible power, immense dangers, unbelievable beauty, and overwhelming forces. I drank the *kava* beside the grave of Paitjom, Winea's most notorious cannibal, who'd eaten more victims than any other man. He was a good and honourable chief who was loved and respected by everyone, and he had the ability to create sunlight and life by manipulating the spirits. When the *kava* made me collapse and allowed my mind to spiral through the different layers of my consciousness, Gramma placed my paralised body directly on top of Paitjom's grave and left me to embrace my fate.

This might not sound dangerous at all, but once I explain more, those of you who believe in the supernatural will be able to appreciate why most villagers die. Over the years, all of the *kastom* men and *matia* have told me that when they connect with the spirits they "*hearem spirit blong bubu,*" (feel their ancestral spirits). This is an accurate description of what happens, because they feel the spirits and never actually hear a voice. While I was unconscious on top of Paitjom's grave, I became empowered with his divine *rapee* and could "*hearem spirit blong him.*" I made a tangible connection with his spirit that was intuitive, and I was filled with knowledge and power that I instinctively knew how to use when I awoke.

To give you a deeper insight into what I experienced, I'll explain how this works. During my travels I've noticed the primitive tribes I've lived with have remarkably similar beliefs and rituals, despite their geographical isolation, and despite them being totally unaware of each other's existence. Their subsistence lifestyles revolve around the seasons and nature, which revolve around the cycle of the planets, which revolve around the sun and the universe. To primitive man, there is a universal connection that makes everything revolve around something. This cycle creates order and stability in a world that's filled with good and evil spirits. It works on the same principle as civilized societies having police, and armies, and governments, to create an acceptable level of balance in everyone's lives.

Man bush believes that even the most insignificant and minuscule aspects of nature have a consciousness, and that these life forces can exist on different planes or can reside within ourselves. The countless atoms that form objects in the natural and supernatural worlds are all vibrating (primitive peoples compare this to revolving) at various speeds and on different spiritual planes. Scientists know that even inert objects do this and that they all contain forms of energy. These vibrations are like radio waves that work on different wavelengths, and our bodies are like radios with tuners. As we've evolved our beliefs and priorities, and our means of survival have changed, so that we no longer need to tune into the supernatural transmissions that we once depended on.

I've been taught that everyone has the ability to connect with the supernatural, but without the essential training and knowledge, we can't safely mediate with the spirits. This ability is just like any other part of our bodies that deteriorates and can become dormant if it isn't used. I call that special factor we all possess, but don't understand, our primal consciousness. Every religion has a different name for our primal consciousness and has its own unique way of accessing or awakening it.

A simple way to make you aware that the primal consciousness actually exists is to use the following example. Nearly everyone has had the feeling that someone is staring at them, and then they've turned around and found out they were right. You don't know how you knew someone was behind you, but you just did. This is a part of our primal consciousness that is still active, and works intuitively as a spiritual bodyguard.

Because it's *tabu* for me to share everything with you, to remove some of the mystery from what I experienced, I'll compare this part of *kastom* with the beliefs of some Hindus, Buddhists, and yoga practitioners. They believe the kundalini runs down our spine, and that it's linked to thousands of centres of energy throughout our bodies called chakras. The chakras are thought to be the equivalent of our spiritual DNA and is what our soul is made from. They vibrate on a lower spiritual plane than our normal level of awareness and can only be accessed by using our primal consciousness, which can be enhanced with exercises, with the right key or knowledge, through the power of belief and prayer, and by intense concentration.

When the highlanders use *kastom*, they open up their kundalini with their primal consciousness to tune into the wavelength their ancestral spirits reside in. As the supernatural energy flows into our chakras, we sometimes feel a shiver up our spine or, depending on the circumstances, we get goose bumps and the hairs on our arms stand on end. The rigid hairs are like an indicator light on a radio that gets brighter when it's tuned into the

Preparing pandanus leaves that will be used to weave a mat. Tabu leaves are used to unlock the primal consciousness.

right wavelength. As your senses become more receptive, and the flow of energy into your chakras gets stronger, this makes the hairs on your arms become more erect.

Our charkas operate on different frequencies, so if an excess of uncontrolled or uninvited supernatural energy flows into them, the effect can be disastrous or fatal. This is how a *kastom* man can kill or heal or manipulate people's lives with black magic. He mediates with the spirits and gets them to direct either a deadly or curative dose of ancestral energy into a victim or a patient. They also use this energy to perform the incredible feats of magic that have been filmed around the world and that have scientists baffled and defy the Western logic that says what humans are capable of doing. These powers can be transmitted world-wide like radio waves.

The highlanders use inherent knowledge, *tabu* leaves, stimulants, and sacrificial human blood and body parts as the key that unlocks their primal consciousness and allows them to connect with the supernatural. If anyone recklessly toys with the spirits without first serving some sort of apprenticeship or initiation under expert tuition to learn how to safely evoke and control these powers, they are risking their lives. I've seen what happens to villagers who have delved into black magic when all they knew was which *tabu* leaves and other ingredients to use. They died or went totally insane, because they didn't have the right preparation or the knowledge to safely handle the supernatural energy. This is known as "the devil turning," which is like short-circuiting a radio with a massive power surge, or like tuning into a wavelength that the radio's components can't handle. When they forced their chakras open, they overloaded their spirit and soul with so much paranormal power that they suffered irreversible damage.

This is why I had to begin the ritual by drinking five shells of potent *kava*. It prepared my senses for the massive amounts of spiritual power that they had to cope with. It also helped to enhance my courage, made me fully appreciate how *tabu* the ritual is, and to a certain extent, it dissolved some of my own self-awareness, so that I wasn't completely overwhelmed by what I was about to endure. A novice would never be allowed to undergo the rite, because even if he did survive it, the effect it had on his mind would probably be too terrifying for him.

When I connected with Paitjom's spirit, his *rapee* gave me a lot of different abilities. He made me fearless and ensured I'd hate our enemies so that I'd protect *kastom*. He filled me with love and inner peace and immense joy, so I could be absolutely selfless, and hospitable, and as good a human being as I can. It also made Paitjom my eternal spiritual bodyguard, which ensures I'll live a long and full life. While I went through this spiritual transformation, I experienced many physical sensations. At times, it felt like I'd been thrown into freezing water or like a massive syringe filled with ice-cold water was being injected into my spirit and soul. This was the equivalent of my kundalini and chakras being opened up and manipulated. Imagine having a drawstring that runs from the top of your head to the tip of your toes, and then having an unimaginably powerful force wrench this down into the ancestral earth. This is what I experienced for weeks afterwards each time the spirits strengthened my bond with our *tabu* ground. Whenever it happened it was so overwhelming it took all of my strength to hide it from others.

Cameraman filmed me collapsing on Paitjom's grave and got enough good footage for our documentary, but he decided not to capture the more graphic part of the rite, as he felt I wouldn't want to see myself in such a traumatised state.

The next morning, for a while I was aware of my surroundings but I couldn't move. It felt as if a part of me had died, but would heal, and it felt like that void in my being had been replaced with bliss and understanding. My consciousness felt like it was in heaven, but my body felt like it was in hell, and it had to suffer a lot more excruciating pain if I was going to survive. I had until nightfall to make it to the other side of the Lappe River, which runs below the climb up to Winea, and is an incredibly *tabu* spiritual safe haven. If I didn't do this by myself, the spirits would kill me, and even if I was carried down it meant certain death, and would cast a huge sense of shame over my bloodline that would follow me through into the afterlife.

Once I started moving, I staggered outside, then I vomited and collapsed. I was so weak and disorientated that I had to drag myself back into the *nakamal* and rest for a while. When I eventually fought my way to my feet, Gramma handed me a walking stick with a sharpened end, and while I staggered and crawled back down to the river he told me to keep the sharp end pointed at my body. This was so I concentrated on staying upright to avoid being skewered. It was much better to risk being seriously injured by the stick than to fail or to receive any help.

I was literally crawling on my hands and knees when we reached the river. When I leapt into the water and swam across to the other side Ravu and the others let rip with a massive yell to express the joy they felt now that they knew their beloved chief and *kastom* brother would survive.

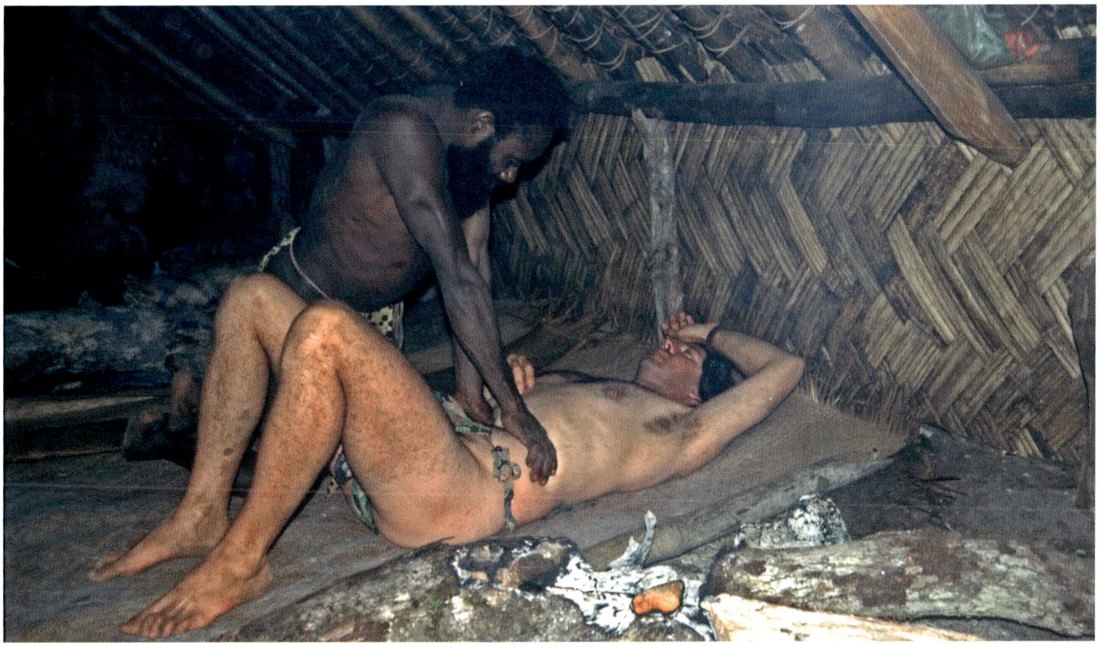

Ravu Magic performing a healing ritual on Rick. Their bond was as close as any brotherhood.

Kastom only required me to cross the river, and although I was beyond exhaustion, I was determined to make it all the way back to our village. Gramma took my stick, and during the torturous trek he whipped the ground alongside my feet to spur me on. When I reached Nukurekum, Ravu and Make performed a painful but very necessary healing ritual on my shattered body.

Whenever I've written that I wouldn't hesitate to kill or injure someone, that was always Tavua talking. Trying to keep Cameraman alive in such unusual circumstances is one of the hardest things I've ever had to do, so when he safely left the highlands after just spending two weeks with us, I felt a huge sense of relief. Then in a secret part of the jungle, away from the prying eyes of the other villagers, I put my whole being to the greatest test when I faced the second and unbelievably brutal part of *Mate Tanatau Maori*. I wish I could explain what I went through but unfortunately it's too *tabu* to share. All of the years of sickness and hardship that I endured were rewarded when I finished my personal journey, and at the end of the *kastom* road, I received the ultimate form of spiritual enlightenment. This is where Paitjom, *Taute*, Gramma, Peta, Busa, and every ancestral spirit gave me the penultimate gift, by obliterating my ego.

Late one afternoon, Gramma led us into dense jungle to look for the hair of a mythical creature that's eluded mankind for millennia. He has an intuitive connection with the animal and went straight to handfuls of thick dark hair that had been shed by a primate similar to Bigfoot called *Podoeka*. Whenever a villager sees the creature it absolutely terrifies him. It grunts and scoffs like a pig and makes so much noise as it crashes off through the jungle that the natives shake from head to toe. Children aren't allowed to go outside a hut at night by themselves because their parents are afraid *Podoeka* will steal them. There are plenty of children from Gramma's bloodline who have been killed by the *matia*, but he's adamant some of them were stolen by a *Podoeka*.

While we were heading back to the trail, Gramma's bowstring snapped, so he took us deeper into the jungle to make another string from the inner bark of a banyan tree. While I filmed him his mood suddenly changed, and for a while, when things got ugly, I thought he was going to hack us up with his machete. He explained later that this was normal.

Because he'd let me film *Podoeka's* hair, the spirits were angry and were trying to turn us against each other. I've experienced the same irrational negativity in other parts of the world when I've documented the sacred beliefs of primitive tribes. This divine intervention is one of the main reasons why outsiders will never fully understand how primitive peoples can manipulate the supernatural. The spirits won't allow it to happen.

Gramma with the wild pig he arrowed during filming.

In a quiet place away from the village, I filmed myself planting a *namele* leaf in soft soil and then Gramma and I unsuccessfully trying to pull it from the ground, but it didn't matter what I did, because the true essence of our primal consciousness can never be captured on film.

For the next two weeks, I filmed *kastom*, rituals, primitive archery, the villagers being shown my compound and recurve bows, and Gramma killing a wild pig with a bow that he made. After I survived *Mate Tanatau Maori* I had another dose of malaria, and by about noon of each day, every fibre of my body felt so weak that sometimes I literally staggered through the jungle or around the village while I tried to film as much as I could.
Following the *kastom* road was never meant to be easy. Most of the time, my search for the answers I was looking for always seemed to lead me down the most adventurous and demanding path, rather than the one that offered the least resistance.

Shower time, Middle Bush style.

Just before I finished filming, Gramma gave me another *Patevina*, which has never been done before. When he passed me the sacred arrow and gave me a shell of *kava* to drink he said, "I gave you many tests while you were very sick with malaria. You completed all of them when another man would've died. Some were too *tabu* to show to outsiders. I trust you because you're strong, and your heart is strong. Your skin is white but you have the blood of a man bush. We will always be one, Tavua. Drinking this *kava* says we are one."

Towards the end of 2006, Gramma is going to sacrifice ten boars with curved tusks so that he can reach his own spiritual nirvana. When the sacred blood of each pig spills onto our *tabu* ground, the powers he receives will also be passed on to me. Then most of the highlanders are going to gather at Nukurekum for a ritual called "*dance fia*" (dance fire). Gramma has asked me to return so that I can dance in the flames of a huge fire with him, and he's given me the right to film this amazing feat, but I have no desire to. I've found what I was looking for and have decided that some things were never meant to be shared with outsiders. They must always remain an enigma.

While science still comes to terms with everything from the natural and supernatural worlds being connected, even the most educated outsider can only guess how the highlanders' primitive mindset functions and how they are able to manipulate and communicate with the spirits. To a *disale*, this will never be crystal clear.

That is the very reason why I risked everything, so I could gain a clearer understanding, and so I could share the answers that I found with you.

Epilogue

We live in an era where technology has surpassed the needs of humanity, but we still can't cater for the basic needs of those who desperately need help. When you think about it, that doesn't make sense.

While I lived amongst the brutality of *kastom* and amongst the discomfort that comes with life in the highlands, I was also shown absolute love and kindness from a people with the most brutal reputation in Vanuatu. When you think about that, it doesn't make much sense either.

Our world is full of contradictions and uncertainty because of who and what we are and because of what it is to be truly human. We have evolved to become one of the few species that feels its survival depends upon slaughtering, starving, suppressing, and manipulating its own kind. When I stepped back through the ages and became a man bush, I discovered that my primitive friends and their ancestors have always shared the same undesirable traits as modern man.

As humanity races towards an undefined goal, and the world becomes a global village, there is one thing about mankind that will never change.

The highlanders taught me that when they let me experience an undeniable proof that the supernatural really does exist and that the human consciousness is eternal.

They were the answers I was looking for.

VANUATU NASONAL KALJORAL KAONSEL
Vanuatu National Cultural Council
Conseil National Culturel du Vanuatu

VANUATU KALJORAL SENTA
Vanuatu Cultural Centre
Centre Culturel du Vanuatu

P.O. Box 184, Port Vila, Vanuatu, South Pacific. Tel: (678) 22129 / 22721, Fax: (678) 26590 Email: vks@vanuatu.com.vu

26th August 2005

Mr Rick Williamson & terence Taylor
Hakatrak Productions & TV3 60 minutes.
Email: ttaylor@tv3.co.nz
Tel:+649366 5913
M:+6421 831 829.

Re: Authorisation to film in Vanuatu on August 26 August to September 23 2005, on the Island Espiritu Santo.

Dear Sir

I wish to inform you that permission is granted to Hakatrak Productions to film a one hour documentary at Winnia village in middle Santo. The crew will document Traditional believes and traditional life at Winnea Village in middle bush Santo on the 26 August to 23 September 2005.

An authorization fee of **100 000vt** for filming fee (one hundred thousand vatu) plus another **100 000vt** (one hundred thousand vatu for deposit of the rush and sign filming agreement before filming commence.. Copies of footage shot including (rush) and edited final copy in broadcast quality **DVCAM OR DVCPRO** IN **PAL** to be deposited to the National Film and Sound Unit at the Vanuatu Cultural Centre. Your deposit fee will be send back to you as soon as we get copies of all the rush.

A representative of the SANMA Provincial Council Mr Christian Maliu a Councilor of SANMA Province will accompany the film crew while shooting as guide, translator at film crew expenses and allowances. He will make sure everything is under control that film crew respect people and their customs taboos.

I would like to give our support of making this film a success.

Yours sincerely,

Jacob Sam Kapere
Head of National Film and Sound Unit.

NASONAL MIUSIUM
National Museum
Musée National

REJISTA BLONG OLGETA OLFALA PLES BLONG VANUATU
The Vanuatu Cultural and Historic Sites Survey
Inventaire des Sites Historiques et Culturels du Vanuatu

NASONAL FILM MO SAON UNIT
National Film and Sound Unit
Service National du Film et du Son

NASONAL LAEBRI
National Library
Bibliothèque Nationale

Glossary

Bobo — The ritual performed after a successful hunt to give thanks to the kastom god and the ancestral spirits.

Bolo — Portions of bamboo about one metre long that are pounded on the ground during kastom dances and singing.

Bubu — An elder, or an ancestral spirit or spirits.

Damate — The supreme devil. A devil that can appear in the guise of a white ghost, a black spirit, or that can become embodied in an animal. The white man is sometimes thought to be a Damate, as is Podoeka, the Bigfoot-type creature that is believed to roam the jungle.

Disale — The white man, despised by all highlanders. Anyone with a light or Caucasian skin tone.

Kastom — The highlander's religion. To perform a ritual is to make kastom. Kastom encompasses all of the natural and supernatural realms.

Lafaet — A feast that is normally held in conjunction with a ritual.

Matia — A cannibalistic and sometimes malevolent kastom man who gains spiritual power by killing and eating a relative or any villager.

Mul mul — A cloth loincloth worn by men and boys.

Nakaimas — The same as a *Matia*.

Nakamal — A sacred hut, used for ritual and where sacred fetishes are sometimes stored. A normal hut can also double as a nakamal. A hut or bar specifically set aside for selling and drinking kava.

Nasara — An area outside a hut where kastom dances and rituals are performed. The *nasara* is always considered sacred ground.

Nul nul — Any club used for fighting. A traditional *nul nul* is shaped like a hockey stick.

Rapee	An object's, person's, animal's, or ancestor's spiritual power. Supernatural power that is similar to mana.
Tabu	Sacred or forbidden. Used to refer to an object, person, area, spirit, or ritual.
Tamamasa	A form of greeting. A way of saying thank you, or expressing something meets your needs, or acknowledging that a situation is fine.
Taute	The supreme God.
Tavue	A sacred conch shell that is blown at the start of a hunt, which is also used during rituals, or to communicate with other villagers or ancestral spirits.

Acknowledgements

Special thanks to Air Vanuatu, Van Air, Ralph Regenvanu, Jacob Sam Kapere, Vanuatu's Museum and Cultural Centre, Vanuatu's National Tourism Office, John Noel and his family, Great Outdoors Camping, Columbia Sportswear, Samick Archery, Sof Sol, Mike Elliot, Sub-A-Roo, Gerber knives tools gear, (See www.gerber.com for more information), Dirty Dog, Lance Bauerfeind, Terrence Taylor (60 Minutes), Cameraman, Connie Wells, James Harvey Mechanical, Brigitte Löcher, Angelika Hörnig, and Murray Crabb Photo Services.

If you liked the book,
then you'll enjoy the DVD

Tavua The White Cannibal

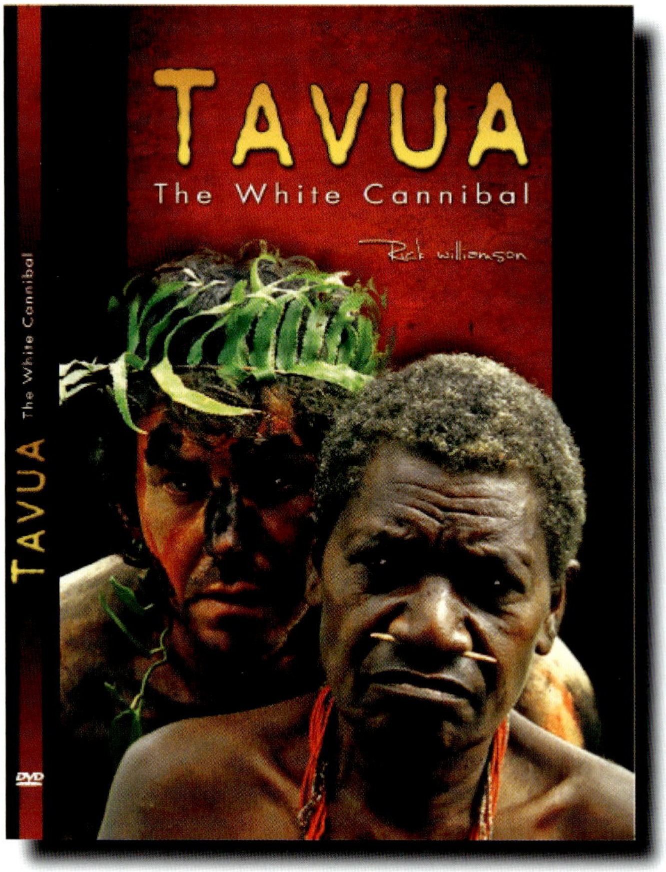

The stunning images and captivating footage provide a graphic insight into the highlander's fascinating culture.

For information on where it's sold, see

www.hakatrak.com or www.bogenschiessen.de
www.archery.de